EVERYONE'S INVITED!

[Interactive Strategies That Engage Young Adolescents]

Jill Spencer

NATIONAL MIDDLE SCHOOL ASSOCIATION
WESTERVILLE, OHIO

Betty Edwards, Executive Director
Jeff Ward, Deputy Executive Director
April Tibbles, Director of Publications
Carla Weiland, Publications Editor
John Lounsbury, Editor, Professional Publications
Edward N. Brazee, Consulting Editor, Professional Publications
Mary Mitchell, Designer, Editorial Assistant
Dawn Williams, Publications Manager
Nikia Reveal, Graphic Designer
Dina Cooper, Graphic Designer
Marcia Meade-Hurst, Senior Publications Representative
Peggy Rajala, Publications Marketing/Ad Sales Coordinator

Library of Congress Cataloging-in-Publication Data
Spencer, Jill, date-
  Everyone's invited! : interactive strategies that engage young adolescents / Jill Spencer.
      p. cm.
  Includes bibliographical references.
  ISBN 978-1-56090-222-5
  1. Active learning. 2. Middle school education--Activity programs. I. Title.
LB1027.23.S597 2008
373.13--dc22
                                        2008032750

Dedicated to

Zachary Reid Hayes and Ella Cresswell Hayes whose curiosity and
sweet natures light up my life. May they attend schools that effectively
and enthusiastically address all their needs.

Meet the Author

Jill Spencer is a consultant and school coach after 30 years as a middle level teacher in Maine. She works with teachers and schools in the areas of middle level curriculum and instruction, literacy, differentiation, technology integration, and building effective leadership teams. Jill was an active participant in the beginning of the Maine Learning Technology Initiative—Maine's laptop program for all seventh and eighth grade students and their teachers—serving on both the design and professional development teams.

Jill is a frequent presenter at National Middle School Association, New England League of Middle Schools, and Maine Association for Middle Level Education conferences and has held leadership positions in all three associations. She is currently a member of NMSA's Publications Review Board.

Jill is passionate about creating learning environments for young adolescents that capture their interest, take advantage of their energy, and help them develop the skills and knowledge necessary for learning in today's—and tomorrow's—schools.

Acknowledgements

First and foremost my heartfelt thanks goes to Ed Brazee, National Middle School Association editor. Ed has been a teacher, mentor, and friend of mine for many years and repeatedly encouraged me to put in writing my classroom ideas, strategies, and activities.

John Lounsbury and Mary Mitchell, the other two NMSA editors, have shepherded this book along, and I am most appreciative for their creative designing of this project. The marvels of video iChatting have brought all three editors into my home for editorial conferences, and so I've had my own individual and personalized writer's workshop.

This book is the result of over 30 years of teaching in the progressive Maine School Administrative District #75, a place where risk taking and collaboration were valued, and innovative teachers were the norm. Many thanks to the superintendents and principals who valued child-centered curriculum and instruction and supported my presenting at various venues. These experiences built my repertoire of instructional strategies, many of which are presented in this book. A huge thanks and special acknowledgement, of course, goes to my colleagues at Mt. Ararat School and Mt. Ararat Middle School. Our many hours of conversation and planning helped me to better understand how adolescents learn. As colleague Sharon Bowman always said, "They have to learn from the inside out!" That imagery really sums up the main idea of this book.

In addition to my colleagues at school, I must acknowledge and thank my colleagues at the Maine Association for Middle Level Education, the New England League of Middle Schools, and Learning Capacity Unlimited. My associates in these groups have stretched my thinking and built my confidence. Thanks also to Andrew Greenstone of Brunswick, Maine, who created Artie the Hapless Anteater and other critters.

Many, many thanks, also, to my wonderful family and close friends who always say, "Go for it!" when I decide to try something that common sense might dictate is not particularly prudent.

Finally, of course, I want acknowledge my students. They always gave me feedback on my instructional practices, and sometimes I was wise enough to take it. —JS

Contents

Foreword   ix

Why You Are Invited—and What's in Store   xi

1. Velcro for the Mind   1

2. Show, Don't Tell—Thinking Processes   13

3. Show, Don't Tell—Procedures   35

4. Build Bridges   43

5. Get Them Moving; Get Them Thinking   47

6. Reading Is a Social Activity   63

7. Rehearse for Success   75

8. Master Vocabulary   85

9. Internalize Concepts   93

10. Check Progress   101

11. Create Connections   107

Before you Leave . . .   113

Fantastic Resources for Putting Zip
Into Your Lesson Plans   116

References   119

Foreword

Everyone's Invited—you and every other middle level educator, parents too—to discover new ways to engage young adolescents in imaginative, interactive learning strategies. Students can also learn here how they can accept further responsibility for their own education, and there are activities in which teachers and students can collaborate in ways that are satisfying and fun.

This is a book that you will return to time and time again, full of inspiring and engaging teaching and learning strategies that are just right for young adolescents. Author Jill Spencer, a highly successful 30-year middle level teacher, uses her extensive knowledge of what works with young adolescents gathered from her own experiences over the years as well as from colleagues across the country, to create a resource that teachers will value.

One of the best aspects of this book, in my opinion, is Spencer's thoughtful use of the word *interactive* to give real meaning to the phrase *active learning*. She establishes these criteria for active learning.

- Each student is involved in the activity or response, and his or her actions are easily observed.
- Students brainstorm, discuss ideas, and problem solve with one another.
- Students, not just the teacher, do the thinking.
- Each student pulls his or her own weight in collaborating activities.
- Students are involved in a hands-on, active manner, well beyond sitting and listening.
- When reading or writing, students interact with one another to clarify and reflect on various ideas.

But make no mistake, while this book contains a plethora of activities that "work" with young adolescents, it is based on solid research as outlined in the introduction. Spencer does an excellent job of connecting the dots to help us understand the relationships between the instructional and assessment strategies presented herein along with the work of Marzano, Daniels, and Bizar, Sprenger, Bloom, and many more. This is a book you can count on.

What else will you love about this book? The bounty of examples that every middle level teacher can identify with, the excellent explanations of strategies and the options for using them in diverse ways, the curriculum applications that pop up when you most need them ... and the "Jill says" words of wisdom by this wise teacher-author who gives bits of advice when it's needed. Finally, another beneficial feature of this book is that Jill has provided you with the actual language she would use with students in conducting many of these activities. These samples of "teacher talk" (shown in italics) give a sense of realism. You would, of course, modify these examples to suit you and your students.

So read, enjoy, and then use these time-tested strategies to help your students become what we want every young adolescent to be—a thinking, engaged, responsible, and happy student. Some day your students will thank you for the guidance you gave them as they became lifelong learners.

Edward Brazee
July 2008

Why You Are Invited— and What's in Store

There are at least three compelling reasons to incorporate active learning strategies into our everyday teaching practices:

- Young adolescents learn best in a kinesthetic manner.
- Students stay engaged when active learning strategies vary the pace and rhythms of a lesson and provide motor breaks needed by these often restless young people.
- Students need to experience concepts in a variety of ways to truly master them, and active strategies provide options.

Further, we know that formative assessments help us make instructional decisions during our lessons on whether to move ahead, regroup, or reteach. Dylan Wiliam (2006) calls these types of assessments that occur within and between lessons "short-cycle assessments"; and some of the most effective ones are active and participatory.

This We Believe: Successful Schools for Young Adolescents (National Middle School Association [NMSA], 2003), the major document presenting the basic philosophy of middle level education, identifies 14 research-based characteristics that exemplify effective learning environments for young adolescents. Five of these characteristics are particularly applicable as guiding principles for the strategies detailed in this book:

- Assessment and evaluation that promote quality learning.
- Multiple learning and teaching approaches that respond to their diversity.
- Students and teachers engaged in active learning.
- High expectations for every member of the learning community.
- An inviting, supportive, and safe environment. (p. 7)

The premise of this book is that each student can achieve at high levels if lessons and units are designed to provide multiple models; time to practice non-threatening, specific feedback; and opportunities to demonstrate learning in varied ways. A sixth characteristic from *This We Believe* is closely related to student achievement: "Educators who value working with this age group and who are prepared to do so" (p. 7). None of the strategies described in this book will be fully effective if students sense that their teachers really don't like them or disrespect their ideas and dreams. The human connection, in my experience, cannot be over-valued!

Learning strategies, however, are only one piece of the puzzle in engaging and motivating students. The most important piece is a "relevant, challenging, integrative, and exploratory curriculum" (NMSA, 2003, p. 19). Learning strategies that actively engage students in thinking about, applying, and demonstrating new learning may make a repetitive, rote, and out-of-date curriculum more palatable to students, but they will not by themselves create classrooms where students soar. The curriculum itself needs to be student-centered, experiential, reflective, relevant, and challenging for students to acquire the knowledge and develop the skills needed in the dynamically changing world of the 21st century. This curriculum must be learned via strategies that engage students and help them build competencies and confidence, directed by teachers who are committed to having each child leave the middle grades with the skills, knowledge, and attitudes that will allow him or her to successfully navigate future challenges.

But just what does the term "active learning," a term used loosely by many, really mean? I suggest that an active learning strategy must meet most of the following criteria:

- Each student is involved in the activity or response and his or her actions are easily observed.
- Students brainstorm, discuss ideas, and problem solve with one another.
- Students, not just the teacher, do the thinking.
- Each student pulls his or her own weight in collaborative activities.
- Students are involved in a hands-on, active manner, well beyond sitting and listening.
- When reading or writing, students interact with one another to clarify and reflect on various ideas.

Of course, active learning strategies aren't the only type of learning that goes on in a classroom. Sometimes students need to read silently, or listen to the teacher, or work independently. Is there a magic formula about how much time should be spent in an active mode? No; it's a question of balance and purpose. It's about the art of teaching—understanding the context of the lesson, the learning needs of students, and how these two factors, among others, interface for optimum learning. The artful teacher knows how to weave active learning strategies into the tapestry of plans for every lesson and unit in a way that provides the most advantageous opportunity for learning that lasts.

During the past 20 years, educational researchers have determined which practices are most effective, and we can use this information to shape our instruction to ensure that each child is successful. Four great sources that summarize recent educational research on learning are

- *Classroom Instruction That Works: Research-Based Strategies for Increasing Student Achievement.* Marzano, Pickering, and Pollock, 2001.
- *Teaching the Best Practice Way: Methods That Matter, K–12.* Daniels and Bizar, 2005.
- *How People Learn: Brain, Mind, Experience, and School.* National Research Council, 2000.
- *How to Teach Students to Remember.* Sprenger, 2005.

These four resources, representative of a large number of such books, provide a road map to use as we craft our plans. Just as a road map shows the best routes to get from point A to point B, these authors point us to the ways that are the most direct routes to learning. Frankly, if this research had been available when I began teaching, I would have been a much more effective teacher. Because I didn't have this road map, I took some very circuitous routes and lost too many students along the way. Fortunately, I also stumbled across some of the strategies that research now supports and thus helped other students make connections and learn new skills.

In the pages that follow, I will show how the major concepts from each of these four books can be applied and support active learning. While the vocabulary and focus from each of the points of view may be different, it is remarkable that the major concepts are very much alike.

Marzano, Norford, Paynter, Pickering, and Gaddy (2001) described nine strategies:

- Identifying similarities and differences.
- Summarizing and note taking.
- Reinforcing effort and providing recognition.
- Homework and practice.
- Nonlinguistic representations.
- Cooperative learning.
- Setting objectives and providing feedback.
- Generating and testing hypotheses.
- Cues, questions, and advance organizers.

All of the active and engaging instructional ideas described in this book fit into two or more of Marzano's instructional practices.

How People Learn, published by the National Research Council (1999) describes the optimum conditions for people to learn. Two major lessons or principles for teachers to act on are as follows:

- Teachers must discover students' "pre-existing understandings" about a topic or concept and use this information to design learning activities. We must know what our students' prior knowledge is and be vigilant in not assuming we know what they do and do not know.
- Teachers need to make visible for students the thinking, reading, and communicating processes that are specific to each discipline. Metacognition is just another way of saying "think-aloud" and is a vital component of learning.

Chapter 1, Velcro for the Mind, explores the importance of prior knowledge and Chapters 2, 3, and 4 are devoted to making thinking processes and procedures transparent for students. Many of the strategies described in later chapters of this book also reflect these principles.

Marilee Sprenger links the latest brain research on learning with instructional practices. She has designed an instructional framework to ensure that students internalize new information and are able to apply it in new situations. Sprenger's (2005) framework, which she calls the 7 R's of the Learning-Memory Cycle includes

- Reach: Engage students.
- Reflect: Provide time for students to think about the new information and make connections to information they already know.
- Recode: Ask students to restate new information in their own words (written or oral) or represent it in a non-linguistic image or physical representation.
- Reinforce: Give feedback to identifies what the learner is doing well and some specific steps to take for improving the quality of work.
- Rehearse: Provide practice time. When learning a new skill, most people must practice 24 times to achieve 80% proficiency.
- Review: Provide a review after the initial instruction, an additional review about halfway through the unit, and then a final review right before the assessment.
- Retrieve the ability to access stored information and apply it in new situations. (pp. 8–10)

In *Teaching the Best Practice Way,* Harvey Daniels and Marilyn Bizar (2005) synthesized the findings of multiple content-based groups such as National Council of Teachers of Mathematics, National Council of Teachers of English, and The Center for Civic Education, and developed a useful list of what teachers should do more of in schools. Many of the items on their list are more curriculum based, and others, such as the five listed below, detail effective instructional practices:

- Active learning in the classroom, with all the attendant noise and movement of students doing, activities and collaborating.
- Emphasis on higher-order thinking.
- Attention to varying cognitive and affective styles of individuals.
- Cooperative, collaborative activity developing the classroom into an interdependent community.
- Delivery of special help to students in the regular classroom. (p. 13)

The five practices highlighted by Daniels and Bizar form a framework of interconnected considerations that must be addressed when developing any instructional approach. Therefore, they are standard components of the strategies described in this book. Many of the strategies that follow are designed to demystify the learning process so that each student can be successful in the regular classroom.

The chapters that follow are full of practical and classroom-tested active learning techniques designed to engage students every day and thus improve their achievement. I adapted some from the ideas of wonderful presenters I have heard at conferences, or authors whose books have become mainstays on my shelves. Most of the strategies, however, come from my own experiences or from colleagues with whom I have been privileged to work over the years. I've tried to be faithful and attribute ideas to their original source; however, the passage of 30 years may have blurred the memories of original encounters with specific ideas and approaches. But whatever the origin, they are all presented here for you to adapt, revise, and make your own.

1...
Velcro® for the Mind

Let's explore ways to build prior knowledge about a topic to be studied. It's important in helping new learnings to "stick."

Because research shows prior knowledge as an integral part of learning, it must play a significant role in lesson and unit planning Some liken prior knowledge to Velcro®, because it acts like the little prongs that grab onto other fabric and hold it close. Prior knowledge provides the miniature prongs that new learning can grab onto as it passes through the brain's intricate circuitry. William Christen and Thomas Murphy (1991), in *Increasing Comprehension by Activating Prior Knowledge*, suggest there are three ways to help students construct prior knowledge: 1) preteach vocabulary, 2) provide experiences, and 3) guide students through a "conceptual framework," allowing them to develop the foundation of knowledge needed in the upcoming unit or reading.

> Research literature supports one compelling fact: what students already know about the content is one of the strongest indicators of how well they will learn new information relative to content.
>
> —Marzano, 2004

Students often possess prior knowledge fraught with misconceptions, and these ideas will be in conflict with information in the unit. Do not expect that merely explaining the correct information will change students' perceptions. A conceptual change should be orchestrated through experiences that help students rework their understanding of ideas, events, and concepts. Think of this change as a rewiring of the brain's circuitry. Interaction among students is vital to the process as they clarify their thinking (Roschelle, 1995). Without taking time to access or rebuild prior knowledge, these misconceptions are never uncovered, new knowledge doesn't make sense within students' mental frameworks, and students fail to internalize new learning.

Accessing and building prior knowledge

Despite the evidence that building and assessing prior knowledge is important, many teachers skip it when they feel pinched for time. Here are several noninvasive strategies that are easy to work into existing plans.

❑ **Centers**— Set up a station in a corner of the room and invite students to explore it when they come in to class or when they finish an assignment. It doesn't have to be fancy, just inviting. We all have students who love to create "stuff." Ask them to make posters or a project board based on the information you provide. If it is a unit you teach every year, have the key materials laminated so you can pull them out and set them up with a minimum of fuss. If the title and some key instructions are in place, you can add new materials as you find them. Following are examples of concepts and visuals for two centers.

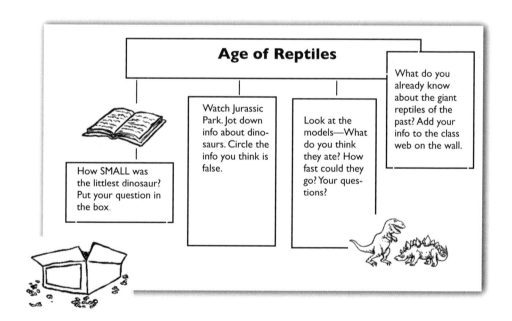

Age of Reptiles

How SMALL was the littlest dinosaur? Put your question in the box.

Watch Jurassic Park. Jot down info about dinosaurs. Circle the info you think is false.

Look at the models—What do you think they ate? How fast could they go? Your questions?

What do you already know about the giant reptiles of the past? Add your info to the class web on the wall.

The American Revolution

Look through these great books to get a taste of our next unit. ↓

Who might not have been happy about the colonies seeking independence? List your candidates below:

_____
_____
_____

Browse:

http://222.pbs.org/ktca/liberty/chronicle.html

1. Look for a topic that you would like to become the class expert on.

2. Jot down any questions that come to mind.

Jill says

Use pictures, books, Web sites, blank spaces for student questions, artifacts, tapes, and videos to draw students to the center. Think about posting provocative questions that relate to both the unit and students' lives. If you have the capacity, think about starting a class blog or wiki to post questions and have students respond.

Here are some sample questions for centers.

- If a meteorite caused dinosaurs to become extinct, could it happen again?
- If the South had won the Civil War, how would our lives be different?
- How much of my 13-year-old brain is still under construction, and what control do I have over making it work really well?
- What are five big ways I might be cheated if I don't understand fractions and decimals?

❏ **Books**— Bring in interesting or thought-provoking books on the topic of the unit, and place them around the room for students to pick up and look at. Have a pile of Post-it® Notes handy so students can mark pages of these books with questions to answer during the unit. Adopt your librarian as an honorary member of your team; librarians are wellsprings of knowledge. At the end of the unit check whether all the questions have been answered.

❑ **Gallery wall**— Designate a wall in your room as the "Gallery of Upcoming Attractions." Post pictures you gather from the Internet and old magazines; better yet, ask students to take responsibility for the wall and have them do the searching and posting. Here's another place to have Post-it® notes handy so that students can ask questions. Incorporating student questions into units builds student interest and engagement.

❑ **Question box**— Use this as a sponge activity at the end of class. Write a series of provocative questions about the upcoming unit and put them in a box. "Can DNA be altered?" "What would be the benefits and the dangers of altering DNA?" "How many times have most of the species on Earth been wiped out?" "What kind of math do commercial fishers use in their work?" "What are some universal causes of conflict?" Pull out one question in the last three minutes of class and have students speculate. Invite students to add their own questions. Be dramatic when you pull out a question. Not your style? Ask a student who enjoys a bit of drama to pick and read the question.

❑ **Children's book**— Read a children's book that relates to the next topic of study. Use the last 3–4 minutes of class for a week. Or ask a student to be the reader. As you read, do a think-aloud—pose questions, identify key vocabulary, explain illustrations, ask for student questions and comments. Keep a chart of vocabulary, questions, and summary statements. You are beginning to help your students build a mental map of future concepts. Listen carefully to comments for any misconceptions students may have so that your instruction addresses those issues.

Even though there is no direct instruction involved, it is possible to use student comments and questions to fine-tune the upcoming unit. Here are three advantages of using such strategies to build prior knowledge:

- These strategies are great motivators because they use student questions to shape instruction.
- These strategies help build student mental maps of important concepts by highlighting key vocabulary.
- These strategies help identify student misconceptions.

Strategies to begin a unit or reading

❑ **Slide show**— Use iPhoto, PowerPoint, Keynote, or other available software to create slide shows that introduce vocabulary, concepts, events, or people to the class. Slide shows help students create mental pictures that they can connect to text later in the unit. . Divide the class into sections and give each section a different role during the slide show. For example, one section can write what they observe, one section can identify and list important vocabulary words, and one can prepare questions the slides raise. At the end of the slide show ask students to share the lists. This is a good point to begin a word wall featuring vocabulary words from the unit.

❑ **Children's books**— Borrow books from the elementary school library or go to the local library for books relating to the unit. Ask the librarians to help round up sources of information related to the unit. Have students read them in small groups, taking note of ideas, vocabulary, and processes. Create and share a huge chart of knowledge for reference as the unit progresses. Model asking questions about ideas and invite students to make their own chart.

❑ **Word sort**— Generate a list of words associated with unit readings. Put each one on an index card and make a stack. Make identical stacks for each group when you divide your class into groups of three or four. Give each group a stack and ask them to sort the cards into groups of words that seem to go together. Groups then label each stack and are ready to explain their thinking. Provide time for each group to share their thoughts.

❑ **High interest article with pictures**— Find a great article on the Internet. Using an LCD projector, share it with students.
  • Stop after the title and do a think-aloud about what the article might include.
  • Look closely at the pictures and generate a list of details together.
  • Read a paragraph and do a think-aloud. What are you wondering?
  • Read some more and invite students to share their thinking and questions.
  • Keep a running chart of ideas, words, and questions.

Jill says

This strategy could work well when coupled with a KWL chart.

NAME _____   DATE _____

KWL Chart

Before you begin your research, list details in the first two columns. Fill in the last column after you complete your research

Topic: _____

1. What do we already KNOW?	2. What do we WANT to find out?	3. What did we LEARN?

Source: Houghton Mifflin Education Place, http://www.educationplace.biz/graphicorganizer

---

Many times students don't have much prior knowledge and won't have anything to put in the KNOW column. With a shared article, students will have information to put in that first column, and that information can serve as an impetus for questions in column 2.

❏ **Movie clip—** Going to show the video version of *Romeo and Juliet* or *Glory* after the Civil War unit? Show a provocative clip before the unit and frame open-ended questions around the clip. Something as simple as . . . "What's going on here?" "Let's make some predictions about what might have led up to this point in the film?" "What might happen next?" "What do you think about this situation?" The clip should somehow connect to ideas that young adolescents feel passionate about—fairness, injustice, search for independence and identity, and others. Film can serve as an emotional entry point to a topic and motivator for students to engage in digging deeper to find the answer to a provocative question.

❏ **Music—** Listening to music and reading lyrics together from a particular era can also be used to develop prior knowledge. Have students work in pairs as anthropologists or CSI detectives to deconstruct lyrics in order to find out what the songs reveal about the culture of a bygone era. Students practice making and checking the validity of inferences as they work through the unit. Keep these ideas visible by posting them on chart paper.

❑ **Internet scavenger hunt**— Set up a portaportal (*www.portaportal. com*) site of links to great sites focusing on your unit. Give students a scavenger hunt based on just those sites. Be sure to include sites with lots of visuals so students can build their background knowledge about the topic through mental pictures. Also, make sure sites are across the gamut of reading levels. Don't forget to check your links.

❑ **Skits and other physical representations of a concept**— Create opportunities for students to represent ideas and concepts physically. These experiences help focus their attention on the big ideas.

Students create short skits based on theme(s) in upcoming units: literature theme (guilt, envy, etc.), math or music (patterns), health (risky behaviors), science (change), or social studies (power).

To get started: Make a list of the themes or concepts in the unit. Make a list of themes in a young adolescent's life and then look for commonalities. The commonalities become the key concepts to address. Here is an example adapted from Beane (1993).

American Revolution	Adolescent Issues
Independence	Identity
Equality	Independence
Taxation	from parents
Power	Fairness
Risk	Risk taking
Interdependence	Friendship
Control of destiny	Changing body

Follow up the skits with free writes, discussions, or illustrations focusing on the concept or theme. The idea is to create in students' minds as many connections as possible between their concrete experiences and the abstract concept about to be studied. Picture a coat rack with hooks (students' brains)—the more hooks (prior knowledge) there are, the more likely the coats (new knowledge) tossed toward the rack will attach themselves to the rack (brain) and stay put (understanding of new knowledge). The brain likes connections.

❏ **A Rube Goldberg contraption**— For a unit on simple machines, direct students to build a series of simple machines that accomplish a simple task in a complex way. Keep it simple with an easy task, limited number of props, and a time limit. Ask students to identify successful strategies that were used in each of the contraptions. Have the class categorize the strategies by similarities and then have them compare their categories to the six simple machines. This type of strategy falls into ABC, CBV approach to teaching science vocabulary—Activity Before Concept, Concept Before Vocabulary. For more information on Rube Goldberg machines, google "Rube Goldberg Machines."

❏ **Habitat observations**— Students record their observations on the flora and fauna for a unit on ecosystems. Have them create mini-murals that illustrate the changes. Post these around the room, and have students do a gallery walk with a partner. Ask them to record their observations: What do you notice? What similarities do you see? What differences do you see? What cause and effect relationships do you notice? Share these observations and then ask students (in pairs or small groups) to make some generalizations based on their shared knowledge. Modeling the process of making a generalization followed with guided practice will be necessary before students can do this activity independently.

❏ **Anticipatory guides**— These activities invite students to think about the content before reading a strategy that has been around for a long time. A series of statements or questions related to the unit or to the reading are listed. Students mark statements true or false before they read and then go back and re-answer the questions after reading. Here is an abbreviated example.

Anticipatory Guide for DNA

DIRECTIONS: Before reading the article, mark each of the following statements true or false in the column "Before Reading." After reading, review the statements and mark them true or false in the column "After Reading."

Before Reading	After Reading	Statement
------	-------	DNA has sugar in it
-------	-------	Cells can duplicate themselves
-------	-------	DNA stands for Double Nucleus Acids

Jill says

Let's kick the anticipatory guide strategy up a notch— and make it more active.

- Label one wall of the classroom *true* and the opposite wall *false*. Write enough statements on oak tag strips so each student can pick one and then go to a wall. Students explain their reasoning and post their strips. Check the postings throughout the reading or unit and move statements to the correct wall. Each student owns his or her own statement and must explain why it moves or stays using evidence from lessons. The students cannot just go willy-nilly down the page marking T or F, rather they must give an accounting of their thinking and listen to others.

- Have students work in pairs or small groups. Give them one sheet with the statements on it, and have them cut it into statement strips. Each group then arranges strips into two columns— true and false. Walk around and probe each group's thinking by asking why they made a particular placement. Then ask groups to star the two or three "trues" they are really sure are correct. Post them with a star for each group that agrees. Go through the same process with the false statements. Now there are two lists on the board—one that lists the items believed to be true and one that lists the statements that many believe are false. Students read with a sense of purpose—to find out if their predictions were accurate.

❏ **At the mall**— Another version of this strategy is called "Tea Party." It works well as an energizer and a way to build prior knowledge.
  - Come up with list of words and phrases associated with the unit or reading—one for each student in the class. Write each on a separate index card.
  - Hand a card to each student and have students stroll around as if they are at the mall.
  - When they hear "stop," they stop and read their card to someone nearby and listen to what that person has on her or his card.
  - Then they start the mall crawl again until they hear "stop," and they read their cards again. (Variation—they can trade cards.)
  - Go through five or six rotations and have students return to seats.
  - In small groups, have them list everything they remember on a sheet of paper.
  - Share the lists and make a big chart with key ideas, characteristics, people, places, and events associated with the next topic. From this chart, students begin to build their mental maps of the topic.
  - Students can also generate questions from these charts.

❏ **Virtual field trips**— Use Internet resources to engage students. It takes time to find the sites and to set up a portaportal site to manage the lesson *(www.portaportal.com)* *(http://del.icio.us/)*, but there are always students who will help you search. Here is just a tiny taste of what is available even to the teacher with a single computer in the classroom.
  - Explore the concept of biodiversity by looking at more than 30 places in the world where biodiversity is threatened. *http://www.biodiversityhotspots.org/xp/Hotspots/*
  - Walk in the footsteps of the victims of the Salem Witch Trials. Travel to Salem, Massachusetts, and visit the sites connected to the Salem witch hysteria. *http://www.salemweb.com/guide/witches. shtml*
  - Gaze on the results of nuclear meltdown. This is the personal Web site of a young woman who explores Eastern Europe on her motorcycle. Her photos and journals open the world of Chernobyl to us all. *http://www.kiddofspeed.com/default.htm*
  - Take your students to the Louvre and visit its many galleries: *http://www.louvre.fr/llv/commun/home.jsp*

Jill says

There is even a Web site that has collected virtual field trips in every content area and has a step-by-step guide for building your own field trip. Take a look at the excellent resource at http://www.uen.org/utahlink/tours/

But gazing at a computer screen, no matter how fascinating the site, can be a pretty passive activity. Structure virtual field trips so that students must think critically and creatively about what they are seeing. Here are four ways to maximize student learning on a virtual field trip.

- Pair students up to explore specific aspects of the Web site and research some of the artifacts, places, people, or eras found there. Have them prepare a PowerPoint using the visuals from the site (with proper citation, of course) to teach their classmates three big ideas from their section. (Here's a great resource by Cliff Atkinson (2005) to help students learn to create PowerPoint presentations that go beyond lists, pictures, and animation: *Beyond Bullet Points: Using Microsoft PowerPoint to Create Presentations That Inform, Motivate, and Inspire.*)
- Craft a provocative question or problem for students to think about as they proceed on their virtual trip. This question or problem should take them into the main content of the unit. Here are two quick ideas. A volcano unit could explore the question "Where is the most unsafe place to live in the United States as far as threatening volcanic action?" Another idea would be to visit Ellis Island to discover similarities and differences between immigration issues during the Know-Nothing era of the 1850s and immigration issues in the early 21st century.
- Have students create their own virtual field trips to share with their classmates.
- Stop the field trip in appropriate places and ask students to summarize what they've seen and heard and to generate some questions to pursue during the unit.

A virtual field trip is a good opportunity to bring the entire team together to view the presentation on a big screen and then differentiate the activities designed for student reflection.

One way to differentiate the reflection activities would be to have those students who would like to create a physical response to show what they learned, go to the science room; those students who would like to journal about what they learned, move to the math room; those students who would like to create a mural, move to the language arts room, and those students who would like to prepare an oral response, move to the social studies room.

After the work in each room is done, bring everyone back together to share reflections. Ask students to listen for common questions or comments across all four groups and then help students synthesize the information by charting the big ideas that were mentioned in more than one group. This approach is another way to help students build their visual, mental maps of key vocabulary and concepts. When they read additional texts, they will have some prior knowledge to connect to the new information.

❑ **Podcasts**— Student interest in the number and variety of podcasts has exploded. Play a podcast at the end of class and use a Ticket-Out-The-Door format to ask students to jot down questions or a quick summary of what they heard. Assign students to listen to specific podcasts as homework, and then the next morning begin class with an activity where students summarize what they listened to the previous evening.

Wrapping it up...

The pressure is on to push. It is tempting just to jump right into the next lesson and begin instructing without taking time to create mental images, introduce vocabulary, provide a concrete foundation for an abstract concept, or even find out what students already know. The reality is, however, that time will be taken—either at the beginning or the end. So, build in time for frontloading prior knowledge, or deal later with frustrated students who have been unable to internalize new knowledge. It's your choice—a lesson or two to up front versus after-school help sessions with cranky students who failed a quiz, left homework undone, or blew off a project. This is one time when it really pays to listen to what research says. Accessing prior knowledge and helping learners connect what they already know to new knowledge improves achievement. Don't over-think any of these activities....*Just do them!*

2...
Show, Don't Tell—Thinking Processes

The well-known Bloom's Taxonomy provides a good way to demystify the thinking process and help students get a grip on what full learning involves.

Benjamin Bloom was an educational psychologist and professor at the University of Chicago during the mid and late 20th century. One of his interests was the cognitive domain, how people take in and process new information. He collaborated with other members of the American Psychological Association to explore the processes of learning, and out of that work came a document often referred to as Bloom's Taxonomy, "a hierarchy of learning." (Chronicle of the University of Chicago). For the past half-century teachers have used the taxonomy as a framework for ensuring that higher-level thinking skills are embedded in their units. Recently, other schol-

> Metacognitive approaches to instruction have been shown to increase the degree to which students will transfer to new situations without the need for explicit prompting.
> —Bransford & Cocking, 2000

ars have revised Bloom's Taxonomy. This revision can be viewed at *http://social.chass.ncsu.edu/slatta/hi216/learning/bloom.htm*. The following strategies are based on the traditional taxonomy.

Designing higher level thinking tasks for young adolescents who still think in concrete terms seems like a conundrum. This challenge is not insurmountable, however, if teachers build a bridge of prior knowledge for students between the concrete application of a thinking skill and its abstract definition. Combining explicit instruction that employs hands-on experiences with metacognitive strategies will help make transparent the thinking processes of the different levels of Bloom's Taxonomy. Don't omit the thinking out loud piece of the instruction. Research on how people learn is very clear about the benefits of sharing the thinking processes involved in a task.

Naturally these demonstrations of thinking processes should not be taught in isolation. Each would be a lead-in to a specific curriculum task. By taking time to teach or reinforce a specific type of thinking, we demystify a thinking process and help our students develop their own mental maps of the components of Bloom's Taxonomy.

Think about how a team could work together to implement a cross-curricular approach to teaching thinking skills! Share the responsibility for direct teaching and reinforcement of thinking processes by mapping out a plan at the beginning of the year. Look at your units to see which type of thinking process goes best with which unit.

Using Bloom's Taxonomy

The illustration at the right shows the six levels of learning and thinking of Bloom's Taxonomy as a stair step leading from the lowest level to the highest levels. Each level is described in a section that follows and a five-step process for teaching is described. The five steps for teaching based on Bloom's Taxonomy are

Steps to higher learning

Step 1   A **student-friendly definition** of the level that describes what students should be able to do with the information they are learning. You will name and define the thinking process in terms students can easily understand.

Step 2   **Key words** characteristic of the level you will explicitly state for students to identify the type of thinking expected in a particular task.

Step 3   **Student tasks** are level-specific suggested strategies that lead to the various levels of learning,

Step 4   A **demonstration lesson** that the teacher can use interactively with the class to model the steps in the processes of the various levels of thinking.

Step 5   A **content lesson** that requires the same level of thinking as that of the demonstration.

Along with the five steps for each level are specific examples, graphic organizers, and references to other resources to get started. Each level's section closes with examples of curriculum applications. By explicitly teaching students about thinking processes and providing them time for multiple practices in an environment free of grading, they will eventually develop the confidence and competence necessary to tackle complex tasks independently.

Jill says Remember: Never , , , never . . . never assess content with a thinking process that the students haven't practiced!

1. Knowledge

Step 1 **Student-friendly definition.** One is able to tell *who, what, where, when, why,* and *how* about an event, idea, or system.

Step 2 **Key words.** tell, describe, list, define, name, collect, find, show, label, recall

Step 3 **Student tasks.**
Identify who, what, where, when, how, and why.
Make a graphic organizer to organize the information you read.
Make a jot list of everything you can recall, then group the items into categories, and make an informal outline.
Color or code similar ideas and details so you can easily refer to them.

Step 4 **Demonstration lesson.** Use Think-aloud strategy or create a board game based on facts from a current unit.

❏ **Think-aloud—** This strategy will be used in every demonstration in every level to model the thinking process for that level. *In order to recall facts, I'm going to brainstorm everything I can remember about _____. I'll write each item on an index card so I can organize them. I like to get all of my ideas out before I do anything else. Organizing facts into categories makes it easier for me to work with them.* (Hint: use strips of paper and masking tape or Post-It® notes to put ideas up on the board; then you can easily move them around into categories.)

Step 5 **Content lesson.** Assign students the same task of creating a board game. *Create a board game (So You Think You Know....) based on facts about today's topic. In order to complete this task, you need to recall as much information as you can about the topic and organize it into a usable format. Follow these steps:*

1. *In front of you is a stack of index cards. Your challenge is to recall as much information as you can about today's topic. Put a different detail on each index card. See how many details you can recall in five minutes.*
2. *Spread the cards out—face up—in front of you. Group them. All of the details in a group should have something in common.*
3. *Label each group with a title that describes what the details have in common.*
4. *Create a paper graphic organizer that will help you keep this information organized. For ideas, google "graphic organizers."*
5. *Create a game using the details you have recalled.*

Curriculum Applications

• Begin each class with a five-minute recall session. Students could web the information or make jot lists and categorize them. A variation is "Ticket in the Door"—hand students a piece of scrap paper and tell them to list five things they remember from yesterday's class. They can work with partners. This will help them recall information and connect the new knowledge from today with what they learned yesterday.

• Allow students to summarize new information. Eric Jensen (1995) in *Brain-Based Learning* suggests that we should take time every ten minutes to review when presenting new material to our students. At a logical time, stop and move to a different part of the room and ask students to take 30 seconds and write down new information they have learned. Have students share and remind them that they are working at the knowledge level of Bloom's Taxonomy. This strategy is a great way to check for understanding. If you are hearing inaccurate information, then you know you need to stop and reteach.

2. Comprehension

Step 1 **Student-friendly definition.** The ability to identify the important ideas in nonfiction and to identify the characters in a story and to follow the action so you know what is happening.

Step 2 **Key words.** explain, locate, summarize, discuss, identify, describe, review, predict, retell, rewrite

Step 3 **Student tasks.**

Pick out the big ideas and several supporting details for each idea.

Retell the story or event from another point of view.

Identify the important people and events.

Figure out the text organizational pattern and use it to find out the author's main points:

Sequence	Description
Cause and effect	Compare and contrast
Chronological order	Listing
Problem-solution	Combination

Step 4 **Demonstration lesson.** (1) Fiction: *Little Red Riding Hood;* (2) Nonfiction: documentary of teacher's choice.

❑ **Think-aloud**— *Whether I'm reading a novel or watching a TV show or video, in order to really understand or comprehend what the plot is about, I need to identify who the important characters are in the story. So let's think about the story of Little Red Riding Hood. (You may have to refresh everyone's memory of the story.) I know that Little Red Riding Hood is a very important character because everything revolves around her—she's on the way to gramma's; she meets the wolf; she almost gets eaten. There would be no story if there were no Little Red Riding Hood. By identifying an important character and being able to explain why she is important, I have demonstrated that I comprehend what this story is about.*

Step 5 **Content lesson.** Explain to the students that another way to demonstrate comprehension of a story is to tell it from another character's point of view. *The True Story of the Three Little Pigs* by Jon Scieszka (1996) is a great model for this activity.

❑ **Comprehension strategy—** Little Red Riding Hood rides again. *With a partner rewrite the story of Little Red Riding Hood from another character's point of view. Your story must use the same chronological order, the same characters and have the same outcome. As much fun as it might be to put in all sorts of detail, you must stick to the basic story because it is for the nightly news and can last no longer than two minutes. Do try to get into your character's mind and show his or her motivation for taking the chosen action.*

Curriculum Applications

• **History class—** Have students think about a historical event as if it were a story. Who are the important people (main characters)? what were the events that occurred in chronological order (plot)? and was there a turning point (climax)? Ask students to retell the event from different participants' points of view. For example, the American Revolution: Thomas Jefferson, King George III, or a Tory who fled to Canada

• **Science class—** Retell the process of photosynthesis from the sun's point of view, the plant's point of view, or the sugar molecule's point of view.

• **Check out the RAFT strategy** for reading and writing—Role, Audience, Format, Task. Google "RAFT strategies" and you will find at least 10 great sites with explanations and examples.

❑ **Think-aloud—** Here's a plan for using a nonfiction source. *A picture is worth a thousand words! That's why documentaries can be so powerfully persuasive. We are going to watch a short clip of _____. Sometimes there is so much information in a documentary or informational text, it is difficult to pick out the important information. Being able to identify the organizational pattern the writer or filmmaker uses will often help. If we know the pattern, we can pick a graphic organizer to help us capture the important information. Let's watch about 10 minutes and see if we can identify how information is being presented to us.*

After ten minutes, stop the video: Looking at our list on the wall of organizational patterns, I'm thinking that _____ is the main pattern. Therefore I'm going to use this graphic organizer to help me identify the important information and increase my comprehension of the big ideas and their supporting details.

Model filling in the important information from the first 10 minutes of the film. *Okay, let's watch 10 more minutes and pay attention to the types of information that are really important.*

Be sure to identify in the video when you should pause to point out the important information and how you know it is important.

Here's your own graphic organizer—let's fill in what we saw that was important.

Common Organizational Structures

- Sequence
- Cause and Effect
- Chronological Order
- Problem-Solution
- Description
- Compare-Contrast
- List

Fill in the graphic organizer together. When you feel students are ready to take notes independently, move on to the independent student task. You still might want to stop periodically and share notes to keep everyone involved.

Independent student task—deciphering documentaries: *As we finish watching the video, fill in your graphic organizer with the important information. At the end I will give you time to meet in small groups to share information, so if you miss something, just leave space to write it in.*

Demonstrate that you comprehend the information in this clip by retelling the important information in your own way with words, pictures, or a combination of both. Use your graphic organizer as a guide.

Jill says

Do not expect students to recognize text organization or patterns (print or digital) without some modeling on your part. Students need to hear you go through a text or video and think out loud (metacognition) about recognizing clues that identify specific text organization.

This chart connects text organization with key words that signal the organizational pattern.

Text Organization Pattern	Key Words	Subjects Often Used In
Description/Listing	next•finally•also•to begin with•for instance•one, two, etc.	social studies•science •language arts•math •family and consumer science•tech ed•art •music•world languages •directions of any kind
Compare/Contrast	however•on the other hand •but also•compared to •in contrast•despite •unless•otherwise	social studies•science •health
Main Points and Supporting Details	evidence•in conclusion •most importantly•first •secondly•finally •of least importance•next	persuasive pieces•essays •editorials
Problem/Solution	therefore•as a result •this led to•if… then •accordingly	science•health•math •tech ed
Chronology	on (date)•before•after•when •first•second•during	social studies•language arts
Sequence	first•next•then•initially,•before •after•when•finally•preceding and following	science•math•art•music •technology
Cause/Effect	because•since•so that •as a result•this led to •consequently	social studies•science •health•math
Question/Answer	author asks a question and then answers	science•health•math •world languages

Teaching text organizational patterns should be shared by all teachers because some patterns are more common in specific disciplines. For example, problem/solution is more applicable in science than in language arts. Interdisciplinary teams across grade levels should map out where the best place is to teach and reinforce particular text patterns. They also should connect with their applied art and exploratory colleagues to discuss ways to support student mastery of this reading skill.

Ultimately we want our students to independently decide the best system to help them identify and record the important information. Studies suggest that the more information students get in their notes, the better they will understand it.

This chart lists sites with lesson plans for teaching the different organizational patterns. The URL's are "tiny" versions of the original Web address. The compacting of the URL was done at http://www.tiny.cc/. You need to click one extra time, but you will get to the correct site.

PATTERNS

Description/Listing	http://tiny.cc/UOPEo http://tiny.cc/cz8yC (art & writing) http://tiny.cc/eLkFw (science)
Compare/Contrast	http://tiny.cc/mrZih http://tiny.cc/7c4D2 http://tiny.cc/07PoP (comparing printed text with digital text)
Main Point and Supporting Details	http://tiny.cc/elMf6 This Web site is about writing an essay but would help in understanding what to look for when reading an essay type of text
Problem/Solution	http://tiny.cc/X6NvD
Chronology	http://tiny.cc/2KukT (PowerPoint of text structures in SS texts)
Sequence	http://tiny.cc/qdbXY
Cause/Effect	http://tiny.cc/pW7Tk http://tiny.cc/ile7f (would need to adapt this one to specific needs)
Previewing text	http://tiny.cc/pTkRA
Other Text Patterns	http://tiny.cc/oUPda (Text from Mt. Everest explorers)

Curriculum Applications

Graphic organizers help with comprehension in every subject. They are online by the hundreds. Google "graphic organizers." Lin Kuzmich (2007) from the International Center for Leadership in Education identified the following graphic organizers as being shown through research to be most effective.

1. Sequence

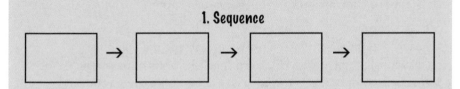

2. Array Web

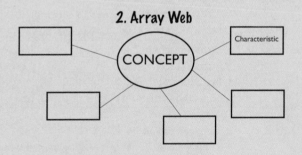

3. T Charts

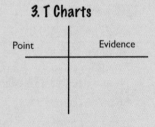

4. Venn Diagrams

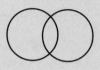 

5. Semantic Feature Analysis

Dessert	Lots of Chocolate	Rich flavor	Creamy	Few Calories
Oreos	√	√		
French Silk Pie	√	√	√	
Fudge	√	√	√	

A good deal of research suggests that American students are rarely asked to process information beyond the comprehension level. The demands of the new century require our citizens to be creative problem solvers; therefore we need to review our units with this in mind. We cannot assume that as our students move into the cognitive developmental stage of abstract thinking that they will automatically know how to apply, analyze, synthesize, and evaluate information. Explicit teaching of these thinking processes is needed.

Step 1   **Student-friendly definition.** The ability to take knowledge and skills learned in one situation and use them to understand or solve a problem in another. For example, when a student doubles a recipe for chocolate chip cookies, he or she is applying skills in using fractions learned in class.

Step 2   **Key words.** apply, model, adapt, change, demonstrate

Step 3   **Student tasks.**

       Give examples and explain why they demonstrate
a concept or idea.
Show how one idea is connected to another.
Use information to solve a problem or describe a situation.
Use methods or theories in a new situation.

Step 4   **Demonstration lesson.** Building a foundation for a
house of cards

       Before starting this activity, have students do a Google image search for foundations. You might try (1) foundations+construction, (2) foundation+bridges, and others. Have students copy 5–10 images to use as models.

❑   **Think-aloud**— *I'm trying to build a tall house of cards, but every time I try to build one it collapses. I think my problem is in the foundations I build. So…I decided to look at some pictures of structures to see what I could learn about foundations and then apply those lessons to my house of cards. Let's look at some pictures together.*
Picture # 1:
I notice that the foundation is as wide as the whole structure.
Picture # 2:
I notice that foundation looks thick. Here are some more pictures.
What do you notice? (List ideas.)
Okay, let's brainstorm some ways we could use these ideas for building a house of cards. Turn to your partner and brainstorm how we might apply what we've learned about building and bridge foundations to a house of cards foundation. Remember in brainstorming, we just get our ideas down and we don't try to figure out which one is best.

Now, let's see what ideas we've come up with. List ideas from class on board. *Right—lots of ideas here. Does any one pop out to us as being really workable?* (Facilitate a discussion of the positives in the list.) *All right—let's put our good thinking to work and apply what we've learned. Here's a pack of cards for each group. The goal is to build a house of cards using all 52 cards. Let's see which group can build the tallest. Who wants to work with me?*

Step 5 **Content lesson.** Last House Standing. *Design and build a house of cards, using all 52 plus the jokers, by applying the knowledge you have about the importance of a good foundation. We'll all fill out the planning sheet before we start.*

House of Cards Activity

Names of architects and builders:

1. Sketch a couple of possible designs for your foundation and house on the back.

2. Give three reasons why your design will work (i.e. how you designed your foundation to be strong or why the placement of the cards is important)

_____

_____

_____

3. Build your house of cards.

4. Think about foundations other than those that support buildings. List below:

5. How are these foundations similar to a building foundation?

Curriculum Applications

At the beginning of the year identify patterns that will repeat. It might be in content—immigration patterns; it might be in processes—writing a good hypothesis or problem-solving strategies. Plan how you can explicitly teach those patterns, and then create instructional tasks where students continue to apply them in new situations.

- *We've studied the reasons people immigrated to the US from the 1600s to the 1900s. Based on what we know, let's apply that knowledge and hypothesize why people want to immigrate to the US in the 21st. century. Then we will research the issue and see if our hypothesis is correct.*

- *We know that non-smoking campaigns have been successful in reducing teenage smoking. Let's look at strategies and then see if we can apply them to a campaign to reduce childhood obesity in our community.*

- *We've used several problem-solving strategies to solve problems in our textbook. Identify a a real-life challenge from our community, and apply these strategies to it.*

Helping students to apply new knowledge in different situations is a key learning strategy. First, applying new skills and concepts in a different context helps individuals internalize new learning. Secondly, students in the middle grades often opt out of learning because they can't see the connections between what they are studying and their current lives. By learning to apply skills and concepts to authentic, real-life problems, young adolescents are more apt to feel their studying is relevant. Therefore they are more likely to participate fully in their classes. We only need to look at the number of teenagers creating content on the web to see that the ability to apply skills in a real-life setting is a powerful motivator for learning how to do something new well.

4. Analysis

Step 1 **Student-friendly definition.** To look at something (a machine, an idea, a plan, an event, set of actions, etc.) and figure out what the important parts (essential elements) are and what their relationship is to one another and perhaps to the world at large.

Step 2 **Key words.** analyze, categorize, infer, examine, compare, critique, contrast

Step 3 **Student tasks.**

>   Look for patterns.
>   Identify parts or properties of the topic or item.
>   Classify.
>   Compare and contrast—Venn diagram.
>   Categorize.
>   Explain with examples.
>   Prioritize from least important to most important.

Step 4 **Demonstration lesson.** Picking the best bike.

>   A real bicycle is an extremely useful prop for this lesson on analysis.

❏ **Think-aloud—** *There are so many choices today when one wishes to purchase a new bike. It we take time to analyze a bike's components and what we want out of a bike, we are much more likely to pick the right bike. Let's start with what we know about bikes We're going to use the same strategy that we used at the knowledge level. We're going to brainstorm things about bikes and sort them into categories like steering mechanisms, gears, and appearance. Working with your group, use the index cards to write down your items, and then sort into categories and label.*

Now let's see if we can create a master chart. (Have chart paper ready to go.) There are lots of ways to categorize, so I'm going to do the first one to get us started—things that make it go. Okay—what are some items you have that go in this category? (List.)
Who has another category that is different from this one? (List and post items. Continue posting categories and items until you have exhausted either your time limit or student ideas.)
We have identified the major components of a bike. That's one of the steps in analysis. Remember, we're going to analyze our data to decide

what is the best bike to buy; so now we need to think about what we want from our bike; we may have more than one thing. It may be both a form of transportation and a way to look cool. For me, I want to get exercise, but I also want to be comfortable. Individually, list what you want from your bike.

Prioritize—another aspect of analysis—your list by starring the two most important ones on your list

As you can see, analysis is a multi-step process. We've identified essential parts, and decided what's important to us by prioritizing different purposes. Now we have to put the two parts together. Look at your starred priorities and the different categories of bike components. Where do you want to spend your money? For example, comfort is a high priority for me, therefore I'm going to spend more money on a soft seat than I am on fancy gears. I've analyzed my needs and the components of a bike in order to make my decision—what about you?

Step 5 **Content lesson.**

Best bike. Write a short description of the type of bike you are looking for. Explain your rationale by describing your priorities and what components you want to spend the most money on.

Internet connection. Give students a budget and send them to bike Web sites to pick out the bike of their dreams and then write up their analyses of why this bike fits all of their criteria. (Substitute ATV's, snowmobiles, or other gear rather than a bicycle for this lesson if that is more appropriate in your community.)

Choosing a Bicycle

I. Identify its parts: (brake, chain, derailleur, handle bars, etc.)

II. Sort the parts into categories: e.g. steering mechanisms, motion, other.

category #1_____	category #2 _____	category #3 _____
1.	1.	1.
2.	2.	2.
3.	3.	3.
4.	4.	4.

III. Identify the purposes for riding a bicycle: transportation, fun, other.

1.   2.   3.   4.

Star (prioritize) the purposes that are of most importance to you.

IV. Think about your *starred* purpose. Which category in #II will be most important (prioritizing) in helping you achieve your purpose? _____
_____

For example: If looking cool is your #1 purpose in riding a bicycle, then an important category might be looks or appearance.

V. Explain why this category is so important to achieving your purpose.

Curriculum Applications

- In a science lab students have to analyze their procedures and findings to come up with their conclusions. Model the analysis thinking process out loud. Then invite students to share their thinking. Create a graphic organizer with key words to help students through the process. Throughout the year, gradually withdraw the supports as students learn to analyze independently. (Hint: the ability to analyze independently will not occur in the first two labs, and students will develop this thinking process at different times and rates.)

- Writing rubrics is a way that students analyze their writing by using criteria set by state and local standards. A Think-aloud is an invaluable tool in this process.

- Looking at artwork or listening to music are other natural occasions to teach students the processes and language of analysis. Model, model, model!

5. Synthesis

Step 1 **Student-friendly definition.** Synthesis is when we combine two or more ideas about a topic from different sources to help us form our own understanding of that topic or come up with a totally new idea. Synthesis is not always about ideas—think of the word *synthetic*. Synthetic materials are made by combining two substances to make a brand new substance that doesn't exist in nature.

Step 2 **Key words.** compose, formulate, create, invent, hypothesize, design

Step 3 **Student tasks.**

> •Combine several ideas to create or design something new.
> •Link ideas from several sources.
> •Predict an outcome based on facts.
> •Add your original ideas to those of others.

Step 4 **Demonstration lesson.** New cookie development

❑ **Think aloud**— *Today we're going to learn about synthesizing. When I synthesize I take ideas from two or more places and combine them. A chef does this all the time when creating scrumptious new dishes. Today we are going to imagine ourselves as pastry chefs, and we are going to create a new cookie. Let's list all of our favorite cookies and dessert bars. I'll go first—chocolate chip cookie—no nuts and brownies—no nuts! (List on board.) Okay, let's see how many cookies and dessert bars we can list in the next three minutes. (List.)*

Now I'm going to ask you to use both your higher level thinking skills and your creativity to create a new cookie. Your are going to use the process of synthesizing by taking ingredients from three of your favorites from this list and creating an all-together new cookie or bar. I would take the chocolate chips from the cookie and the chocolate chewiness of the brownie and combine them with . . . oh I don't know, I'll think about that while you use this graphic organizer to help you with a new recipe that synthesizes old ideas into something new.

Step 5 **Content lesson.** Creating the perfect new cookie.

1. Name your three favorite cookies or dessert bars (brownies, date bars, chocolate chip cookies)_____
2. Now, list their ingredients.

3. Look at the three columns of ingredients—obviously you think these are yummy! Combining any of the above ingredients, create a new, original cookie or dessert bar.

Jill says

A NEW IDEA based on combining OLD IDEAS makes sense!

Curriculum Applications

- Current events: have students read an account of an event and also watch a news account of the same event. Together create a Venn diagram of how the two accounts are similar and different. Individually have students write a summary of their understanding of what actually occurred. Great resources: *www.newseum.org*—where newspapers from around the world are online every day.

- Research the topic of synthetics so students are able to explain how a new substance is made from two or more different substances.

- Have students read different texts on the same topic (any subject) and have them write short summaries of what they know about the topic. Have them analyze each other's summaries to make sure they include ideas from both sources. Use different-colored felt markers to code the sources.

6. Evaluation

Step 1 Student-friendly definition. When you evaluate something, you examine it carefully in order to judge its worth or value.

Step 2 Key words. assess, choose, determine, select, justify, verify, support, rank, recommend, judge

Step 3 Student tasks.

- Create criteria to use to judge the value (make a chart).
- Compare to another similar idea or object and determine which is better.
- Double check to see if opinion or fact—look at the evidence.
- Make a choice and back it up with specific reasons.

Step 4 Demonstration lesson. Select criteria for picking the best band.

❑ **Think-aloud—** Model your thinking. *Lots of times in your life you are going to have to evaluate a situation or a potential purchase and decide which provides you with the best value—financial, emotional, happiness, or other. We are going to explore a process you can use in a multitude of situations in which you use criteria, compare items according to that criteria, and leave with reasons to back up your decision. We're going to create a matrix. We will evaluate music groups—bet you all have an opinion on that topic. Let me model what I mean about criteria—concert tickets cost big bucks, so before I'm willing to spend that kind of money, the musical group has to meet my criteria. Here's mine: I have to recognize the songs, I have to be able to sing along, I have to be able to make a comment to a friend during the performance without shouting, and I want to leave the show humming. So, the Kingston Trio, Manhattan Transfer, and Bob Dylan all fit my criteria.* (Hint: obviously any criteria and groups can be used in the Think aloud—the point is for the students to see and hear the process.)

When you stop laughing at my criteria, you can have a go at deciding which band is best. But instead of trying to shout each other down, you will be able to present your case with evidence to support your stand. Work with a partner through the process to develop a criteria matrix. Maybe we better make sure everyone knows what criteria are—who can define that word for us?

Step 5 Content lesson.

1. In your group, brainstorm what makes a music group good.

2. Now prioritize—everyone in the group gets to star (*) the three characteristics he or she thinks are most important. The five items with the most stars are your criteria for judging.

3. Make a chart. Your criteria for determining a great group goes across the top—one per box.

4. Select groups you want to compare.

5. Use a 1–5 scale to rank each of the criteria: 1=low, 5=high

6. Fill in the chart—together or separately.

7. Total scores; prepare your report for MTV to explain your choice and criteria.

Group	Criteria 1	Criteria 2	Criteria 3	Criteria 4	Criteria 5	Total Points

Curriculum Applications

- This type of chart could be used as a prewriting strategy for a persuasive piece—most effective energy source, best Civil War general, what makes an effective president—the list is endless.

- Students can be taught this process for decision making in advisory groups, student council, or when they have to choose topics for a long term project that will take time and energy.

Wrapping it up...

Gone are the days when just brawn could provide a steady and reasonable income for a large portion of our population. Twenty-first century adults need the capacity to continue learning new information and skills and to be flexible and adaptive thinkers. Creativity and problem solving or what we used to call "Yankee ingenuity" (in least in my part of the world) will continue to be integral to a vibrant economy and culture. These skills and habits of mind will not burst forth fully formed from an 18-year-old's brain without incubation throughout his or her pre-K–12 education experience. Since our students' problem-solving and reasoning skills are just emerging, we have an obligation to help them learn to think critically. We want all of our students to be successful in college-prep and challenging career-prep courses so that they have true choices when they graduate from high school. Taking the time to provide concrete learning experiences that develop thinking patterns must be integral to our curriculum and instruction. ...*Remember, we are trying to build lifelong learners.*

3...
Show, Don't Tell—Procedures

Here are a few procedures students can master as they are learning how to learn.

Lack of confidence in their abilities to independently carry out a process or procedure often gets in the way of students' learning. Teachers who model non-threatening practices of procedures help students internalize a procedure or process so that they can eventually use it independently and thus concentrate on the new content.

❑ **Pop media** is a tool for teaching students how to approach specific writing assignments. On the next page is an example that uses a comic strip to model the thinking necessary to delve into text or extract from a film or a play many details about a character and his or her personality. You will follow the adventures of Artie the Hapless Anteater, but any comic strip will do.

Start the lesson by asking students to describe Artie physically. As they do, list the words on a chart. Without a doubt the word *fat* will come up—a great chance to work on synonyms and antonyms and positive and negative connotations (pleasantly plump and obese). Someone else will note that he has big eyes. A prompt such as "What do they remind you of?" allows for a quick review of similes and metaphors. "His eyes are two golf balls perched on an elephant nose."

After creating a list of descriptive words about Artie's physical appearance, it's time to do another list describing his personality. It's important to emphasize that students should study what it is that Artie says and does that gives clues about his personality. For example, a student might say, "He's trying to be cool." A prompt of

"How do you know that?" might bring the response, "He's wearing his baseball cap backwards." To avoid having the classroom dialogue be just between teacher and one student at time, have students pair up and have a little contest to see which pair can come up with the most descriptors or the most unique ones.

Created by Andrew Greenstone

The next step is to model how to take these pre-writing lists and turn them into paragraphs. Using models, writing a character description together on the overhead or computer, allowing students to work in pairs, or putting work up either on chart paper or the LCD projector are all ways to allow more reluctant writers to see how other writers put ideas together. "Make thinking transparent" is a valuable strategy to use when students are mastering a process.

Why not just go through the entire process the first time with the assigned novel, text, or film and skip the extra step you might ask? The mix of image and text makes the information more accessible to each student and therefore more likely that everyone will engage in the lesson. Young adolescents easily relate to pop culture, and that can be an effective tool in teaching ideas and processes.

❑ **Visual scaffolds**— Charts and posters provide guidance for students as they work on an assignment by listing steps or things to include in the assignment. These visuals are helpful to students for a variety of reasons. Visual cues are appropriate for visual learners and for learners with receptive and expressive language challenges. The organizing format is also critical for disorganized or unsure learners and the young adolescents whose language centers of the brain are still under construction.

Here is a chart—a visual scaffold—that might hang in a science laboratory describing parts of the activity. How could it be adapted to any classroom?

Science Lab

Components	Guiding Questions
Title	What's the subject of the lab activity?
Problem	What is the purpose of the lab?
Hypothesis	What is your prediction? That is, what do you think will happen when you run your experiment?
Experiment	What materials will you use? What will your procedures be? Do your directions make it easy for someone to replicate?
Data	What are the results? Will you use charts, graphs, spreadsheets to record your data? How often do you need to check or collect data?
Conclusion	What do your results mean? How do your results relate to the problem and hypothesis? How will you analyze the data? How do you know your data are valid?

The chart is a great reference for students, and the science teacher has carefully explained and given examples of each component. And yet ... the lab reports produced by students are disappointing. One reason that the work is not up to the teacher's expectation is that the students haven't really internalized the attributes of each component. A few targeted active learning experiences will help students develop the skills needed to improve their lab reports.

❏ **Extended Think-Pair-Share—** This strategy will help each student in the class develop a common understanding of a concept, term, or process. Think about the word *hypothesis*. Most students can give an approximate definition, but probably not a concise one in their own words. Use the steps below to help each student really understand what the word means as they participate in a multi-step clarifying process.
  - Have each student write down his or her own definition or understanding of *hypothesis*.
  - Pair up the group and have them share their ideas. Each pair then writes a definition they both agree is satisfactory.
  - Each pair joins another pair. They share and discuss their definitions. The group of four then collaborates on a definition they all support.
  - Each foursome joins another foursome. They share and discuss their definitions. The group of eight then collaborates on a definition as before.
  - As the groups get larger, it is important to monitor time and conversations carefully. If groups get bogged down, they might need a bit of coaching.
  - Depending on the time frame a group has for this process, keep combining groups to further refine their understanding of the term "hypothesis." The ultimate goal is to continue combining pairs until there is just one group and one definition. Occasionally, time constraints prevent this outcome.

At whatever point the process must end, save time to write out the final definition and post it for future reference. In addition to developing a common understanding of a term, this process also demonstrates to students that their thinking is valued.

❏ **Critic's corner**— This strategy helps students identify critical elements in any type of writing. In this case we will use science lab conclusions as the example.

- Write a science lab conclusion (or any other type of writing typically assigned) that is way below standard.
- Using either an LCD projector or an overhead, project your sample for students to critique. Make sure the font is big enough for the last row of students to read easily. Providing photocopies will ensure everyone can easily read the text.
- Review the criteria for a good conclusion.
- Pair up students and have them identify the good elements of the conclusion.
- Have students share and discuss their findings.
- Have pairs identify the elements that are missing or need improvement..
- Share and discuss.
- Ask the pairs for their findings.
- Thank students for their feedback and promise to bring a revised conclusion to the next class for further feedback. You are thus modeling the process of giving feedback and improving quality, which is just what you want them to do in their own work!
- Provide a revised conclusion the next day and ask students whether it meets the established criteria.
- Use a Think-aloud to share what you thought as you revised.

Jill says

Your students may send your conclusions back. You never know!

❏ **SOAPSTone**— Here's another wonderful visual scaffolding device developed by Tommy Boley of the University of Texas at El Paso to help students analyze text. It's often used in Advanced Placement (AP) and pre-AP courses. Gayle Gregory and Lin Kuzmich (2005) in *Differentiated Literacy Strategies for Student Growth and Achievement* cite it as a way to analyze different media presentations (p. 143).

SOAPSTone Organizer

Components	Guiding Questions
Speaker	Whom does the author represent, himself or herself? A specific group?
Occasion	Why is the author creating this piece? Is she or he providing an emotional response based on data or a reaction to an event?
Audience	Who is the intended audience? How does the audience affect the author's presentation?
Purpose	What does the author want the audience to think, or feel, or do?
Subject	Can you write a one-sentence summary of the subject of the piece?
Tone	What feeling do you get when you read this piece? How does the author use word choice, images, and organization to achieve his or her purpose?

An active learning strategy that will bring this scaffold to life is a Carousel, which asks students to think of different examples for each of the terms and should be done as an introduction to the SOAPSTone organizer.

❏ **Carousel—** This strategy gets students moving around and talking to one another.
- Post charts around the room with a different SOAPSTone component term on each one.
- Divide the class into groups of 3–5 and give each one a different color marker.
- Start each group at a different chart.
- Give them three minutes to list as many real-life examples of the term as possible, e.g., audience: peers, family, friends, church congregation, newspaper readership. Some Carousel prompts are

- What types of groups might an author represent? Senior citizens? Farmers?
- What are some emotional responses an author might want to generate?
- What kind of actions might an author want his or her audience to take as a result of reading the text?
- At the end of three minutes have students rotate and add additional examples to the next chart.
- Rotate the groups through all of the charts and review them with the entire class.

All the different, authentic examples generated by multiple interactions will engage students and help each one internalize the meanings of the terms.

SOAPSTone could be used in many content areas as a scaffolding device to help students react to and analyze text and media. Imagine the degree of competence and confidence students would develop if this approach were taught and reinforced across the curriculum and grade levels. They would have many chances to develop their analytical thinking abilities and improve their writing. SOAPSTone may not appeal to everyone, but the idea of a school-wide scaffolding device to help students develop these skills is a powerful concept and is easy to implement.

Wrapping it up...

Young adolescents, especially males, would do almost anything to avoid looking stupid in front of their friends. Too often this attitude gets in the way of developing skills that lead to increased achievement and learning. We have the power to create a classroom atmosphere that makes it okay not to be perfect on the first or second or maybe even the tenth try. Non-threatening (ungraded) practices build students' understanding of the steps necessary to complete a task. These practices conducted in a warm, relaxed, but focused situation will help students develop the confidence needed to tackle content tasks that previously appeared daunting. It takes up-front time to plan and implement these lessons, but it saves time that might be spent in detentions, extra-help sessions, or calls to parents about missing work. Teaching is not about catching students making mistakes, but rather providing scaffolding for learning that can be eased away as students gain mastery. ...*Atmosphere and opportunity go together to support learning.*

4...
Build Bridges

Middle grades students can grapple with abstract concepts, but they often need a concrete "bridge" to help them along the way.

Sometimes a term in a process or a procedure comes along that is so abstract it gives students pause when they try to define it. When students do the SOAPSTone activity, it is hardest for them to define "tone." Several suggestions follow that address the reality that in any class of middle grades students, there is a spread along the continuum from concrete to abstract thinking skills.

When an abstract concept is difficult for students, bridges must be built for them between what they know—the concrete world—and the abstract. These bridges allow each student to create and refine an accurate mental map of ideas and concepts that will act as a foundation on which to construct new learning and understanding.

Bridges to connect the concrete to the abstract

Three examples of strategies that will make the needed connections are provided in this brief chapter.

❑ **Digging deep for meaning—** This strategy starts with a familiar situation from students' lives and adds descriptors related to an abstract idea or concept.
- Brainstorm familiar examples where a concept or term is played out. Using literary tone as an example, requests for accepting late homework, ordering a sibling out of your room, text-messaging friends—all require a different tone. Write each one on a slip of paper.
- Divide the class into small groups. Have each group pick one slip and then create a skit with dialogue appropriate for that situation.

- As the first group performs for the class, ask the other groups to think about what message the speakers want to convey, the emotions involved in the dialogue, and what words and gestures are particularly effective.
- After the first group performs, model your own thinking about the word "tone," using words of the speakers as evidence. Ask students to add their own thinking.
- Keep a two-column chart: the left column for the different types of tones portrayed; the right for the words and gestures that give evidence for the tones.
- Have other groups perform their skits and repeat the discussion process.
- At the end of this activity, there is a class wall chart with several concrete examples of tone and of the types of language that illustrate each different tone.

It's often difficult to identify these connections on the fly. Use team time or content area meetings to review upcoming units and brainstorm a list of concrete connections to which young adolescents will relate and link them to the major unit concepts. This activity is a great investment of 10–15 minutes.

❑ **Connect 4—** This strategy, like the game Connect 4, looks for ways to make connections. For this strategy to work, teachers must collaborate to help their students grasp concepts.

Think about the concept of variables. Students often have a difficult time understanding that "n" can stand for any number in an algebraic expression or equation because they haven't really internalized the concept of variable. The math teacher can ask teammates or others in the building to help by taking a bit of time to explore the concept of variable in their disciplines. For example, the language arts teacher might use short story plot lines as the constant and then demonstrate a variable by discussing how the different plot elements vary and change the story. The woodworking teacher might talk with students about how materials are a variable in furniture making. This week it might be the math teacher asking others to help students gain a broad-based understanding of the concept of variable, and next week it might be the science teacher looking for help with the concept of systems.

Have fun with this strategy; announce the *Week of the Veritable Variable* or *Slimy Systems* or *Pitter-Patterns* and set up a few short competitions for homeroom or advisory time as well as work on the concept in classes. The competitions might include these challenges.

- *In three minutes, list as many different types of patterns that you see in this room.*
- *In all of your classes, listen for the word "system"—note any references. Bring your list back to homeroom tomorrow and enter it in a drawing for a prize.*
- *Write down your schedule for your entire 24-hour day and circle the items that you consider variables. Compare lists. Who has the most variables? The least?*
- *Design a logo for the concept of the week that captures its meaning.*

The teacher who owns the concept will naturally be tying together the strands from the different classes and activities in his/her classroom. Here's a short list of concepts that span discipline areas:

scale	diversity	model
cell	expression	movement
action/reaction	system	quality
interdependence	energy	structure
tone	change	symbols

A concept doesn't have to apply to every discipline for this strategy to work. What is important is that students have multiple exposures and practices with a concept so that its abstractness is diminished and student understanding of its authentic applications grows.

❏ **Concept bingo—** A combination of scavenger hunt and bingo, this strategy uses the eight multiple intelligences to explore a concept.
- Create a 3 x 3 grid (larger will work too) and fill in each spot with a task related to the concept.
- Each task should also tap into one of the multiple intelligences. It's not necessary to have a task for each intelligence; it's better to have authentic tasks than ones that are a real stretch.

linguistic	logical-mathematical	spatial
bodily-kinesthetic	musical	naturalist
interpersonal	intrapersonal	

The following is an example of a grid for patterns that includes all the multiple intelligences.

Find someone who has a pattern on his or her clothing.	Find someone who can sing or whistle a tune that has a pattern.	Find someone who can demonstrate a dance that has a pattern.
Find someone who can fill in the correct numbers in the following pattern: 2, 4, _ 256, ___.	Find someone who can describe a pattern of behavior seen in our cafeteria.	Find someone who can draw a fractal on the back of the grid sheet.
Find someone who can describe a pattern in his or her own life.	Find someone who can list five things that have patterns.	Find someone who can recite a poem that follows a pattern.

- Give students a grid sheet and have them find classmates who can perform the different tasks.
- Students must ask their classmates to demonstrate the tasks before they fill in the grids with names.
- Award a prize for the first one to gather the required number of names. Hold students accountable by asking them to demonstrate that they can complete the task.

Wrapping it up...

What concepts in middle school were difficult for you to grasp? The difference between simple interest and compound interest confounded me in seventh grade. Perhaps some experiences using Monopoly® money would have helped me understand the concept more quickly, and the formulas for figuring out the interest would have made more sense. Concrete experiences in a variety of contexts help everyone make sense of abstract ideas. It is doubly important that we provide these experiences for young adolescents who are making the transition from concrete thinking to the abstract. Many will still be in the midst of transitioning when they leave eighth grade for high school. This situation does not mean that the only kind of work middle graders should attempt is recall. It just means that we have to carefully craft lessons that connect the abstract and unknown to the known and the concrete multiple times across the curriculum. Offering support when students stumble and struggle with a concept after several lessons helps too. We then have to find one more way to connect the concept to something from the students' lives. . . . *It's hard, but important work!*

5...
Get Them Moving, Get Them Thinking

Combining physical movement with creative thinking activities just makes sense when working with these anxious-to-be-active young adolescents.

This chapter has strategies you will want at your fingertips, but there are too many to remember. A suggestion then—devise an organizational system that allows you to browse quickly for an idea:

- A notebook with a different page for each strategy.
- Punched index cards threaded onto a large ring with notes describing the strategy.
- Digital spiral notebook created in NoteShare (*www.aquaminds.com/*) that automatically creates a table of contents and index.

Choosing partners or groups

Many action strategies require working with a partner or in small groups. Here are several ways to form groups in classrooms. To begin with, make sure students understand they will work with one another for short amounts of time over the semester and that the groupings will change regularly. Sometimes students will work with a good friend, other times with acquaintances, and other times with people they really don't know—or in various combinations. Here are five good ways to establish groups.

❑ **Fold the line—** Have students line up in a straight line according to a prompt. Have the end person on the right walk down and face the end person on the left. The rest of the line follows so everyone is standing across from another person—you've folded the line. You can then divide the line any way you want to—establish partners, groups of four or groups of six. Here are three possible prompts that result in a straight line with everyone facing the teacher.

—Months of birthdays: January babies start here, and the line ends with December babies.

—Hot, spicy food: At this end of the line are folks who love hot, spicy foods; at the other end of the line are people who love foods like mashed potatoes—no spice at all. Decide where you fit along the line according to your food tastes.

—Vacations: On one end of the line are those who would rather laze around on a beach, and on the other end are those who would rather ride their mountain bikes down a challenging track filled with large trees and very hard rocks.

❏ **Playing cards**— Figure out how many cards you need for your class and whether you want partners or groups of a particular size. Same red numbers (e.g. 7 of hearts and 7 of diamonds) are partners, or all of the sevens are a group. Shuffle the deck and let students pick one, or deal them out.

❏ **Music partners**— Make a 4 x 4 grid and duplicate enough copies for every student. In each space write the name of a different type of music: rap, folk, R & B, gospel, rock, or heavy metal. Have students go around looking for other students to sign their different squares. Remind them if Sally signs Alberto's rock and roll square, then Alberto must also sign Sally's rock and roll square. Make sure the grids go into a classroom folder where they will always be at hand. Now you have ready-made partners—*Today I want you to meet with your folk music partner.* The information in the grid could be any-thing—sports or sports teams, types of rocks or clouds, or countries of the world.

Rap	Rock & Roll	Gospel	Classical
Rhythm & Blues	Jazz	Broadway Musical	Heavy Metal

❑ **Turn to your neighbor and share—** When you simply want students to have a quick discussion or share an idea, just have them turn to someone near them.

❑ **Go togethers—** Create a list of items that go together: salt and pepper, Romeo and Juliet, or Minneapolis and St. Paul and put each item on an index card. (Have your students generate the list of pairs and ask for volunteers to make the cards.) When you need partners for the day's activity, shuffle the cards and distribute. Students then find their other half. This method provides a good stretch break if everyone has been sitting for a while. Here are some variations:
  • *Puzzle pieces:* cut index cards into two pieces in a jigsaw format. Students find the other half of their puzzle piece. You can also use three- or four-piece puzzles.
  • *Picture pieces:* collect interesting pictures and cut them up like a puzzle—in sets of three, four, or more pieces. Students find the rest of the picture of which they have one piece. If the picture relates to the topic under study, their first task might be to identify the picture and explain why it is important.
  • *Animal noises:* (Use this idea only if you have a high tolerance for giggles.) Write animal names on index cards—if you want partners, you'll write the name two times, if you want small groups, write the name three or four times. Shuffle and distribute the cards. Students find their partners or group by walking around imitating the animal by the noise it makes. Lions identify themselves by roars. Obviously, you need to decide if this strategy is appropriate for your class, in your section of the building, and with the understanding of your colleagues next door.

Making direct teaching more interactive

When using a direct teaching strategy, it is important to keep students engaged and to check for understanding of the ideas and concepts presented. Eric Jensen, a leader in brain-based learning, claims that it is imperative to review new information every 10 minutes, again within 48 hours, and once again in seven days. These reviews help students internalize new information. Following are several review strategies to use in each of the time periods.

10-Minute Review Strategies

Keep these reviews lighthearted and tension-free. The point is not to catch someone not knowing, but rather to check for understanding so you can make adjustments in the next section of the lesson and also for students to summarize and hear others' thinking. Summarizing and metacognition are two major elements of increasing learning.

❑ **Turn to your partner and share**— The class should be divided ahead of time into partners with each partner designated either A or B. Then at appropriate times during the lesson, ask the students to turn to their partners and share: For instance,
  • Partner A explains the Federalists' take on trade, and then partner B shares the Jeffersonian Democrats' views on trade.
  • Partner A explains what the subject of this sentence is, and then partner B identifies the verb.

❑ **Everyone up**— Ask all the students to stand up—they get to sit down when they can share one fact, idea, or new vocabulary word related to the lesson. Always call on your reluctant learners immediately if you see their hands go up—build a positive connection with them and acknowledge they have a correct answer. Never have a stare-down contest with students who aren't raising their hands— just look at the clock and say, "We're out of time! Everyone else sit down." Even if students haven't shared they've heard ideas restated and summarized. (This strategy was developed by a high school English teacher in South Portland, Maine whose name, unfortunately, I never knew. I've shared it widely, and teachers have adapted it in a variety of ways. So can you.)

❑ **Take five**— After 10 to 20 minutes of direct teaching and note taking, take a break from teacher talk and allow the students two to five minutes to share their notes with a partner and fill in any missing information or correct any mistakes. Encourage students to note questions they have on note cards. Walk around, collect cards, and use these student questions to help you frame the next 10–20 minutes of direct teaching. Anonymous questions on note cards are a way for students to ask questions while avoiding feeling stupid in front of their classmates. Also encourage students to e-mail you questions for the same reason.

❏ **Small group brain drain**— If the class is sitting in table groups, have chart paper and markers at each table. After 10–20 minutes, ask groups to list everything they can recall and underline the three most important things. Again, this gives you a quick view of level of understanding as students talk about ideas, identify the most important ones, and see these ideas restated in different ways. A variation is to ask the groups to use images to represent the three big ideas. Using "non-linguistic" representations of information is a proven way to increase learning (Marzano, Pickering, & Pollack, 2001).

❏ **Building shared understanding**— This is adapted from a Spencer Kagan strategy). With four heads collaborating, the task is quite manageable.
  • Students are in groups of four with one whiteboard for the group.
  • Each student has a number from 1–4.
  • Explain that each group must figure out the answer together.
  • Each group must ensure that everyone understands the answer and the process the group used to reach it, because the teacher will call a number 1-4 and the person with that number must explain the group's answer.
  • Project the question and give groups time to work together as you walk around monitoring and coaching.
  • Call time when all the groups are ready and ask them to hold up their answers.
  • Peruse the answers, but don't indicate right away which are the correct ones.
  • Call a number from 1–4 and ask those students to stand up.
  • Ask these students to explain their group's answer.
  • Take time to process the answers, and help those groups who didn't come up with the correct answer figure out where they went wrong. Understanding one's mistakes is as important as getting the correct answer.

❏ **Exit slip**— This strategy is also known as Ticket-Out-the-Door or Passport. During the last five minutes of class, ask students to summarize the learning for the day. Two examples follow:
  • 3-2-1: Write three facts about Thomas Jefferson, two controversies between the Federalists and Democratic-Republicans, and one similarity between the Jeffersonian era and our own.

- Write a 25-word summary or draw a cartoon that captures the big ideas we discussed today.

❏ **First one out the door**— *Who wants to be the first one out the door?* Hands shoot up left and right. *Okay, to be the first one to line up at the door you have to answer a question.* This strategy makes good use of the last couple of minutes of class. Here's how to orchestrate this activity. Five minutes before the bell rings, ask the question "Who wants to go to lunch first?" Have a series of questions that summarize the topic under study ready to ask. As a student answers the question correctly, she or he gets to move to the door. Alternate between boys and girls as you choose students to answer. Make sure those lined up at the door do exit first when the signal is given!

48-Hour Review Strategies

These strategies are going to take a bit longer than the previous 10-minute strategies, go a bit deeper into the content, and thus should require a different level of thinking than just recall. You may ask students to find similarities and differences, summarize, or perhaps apply or synthesize information.

❏ **Physical Venn diagram**— A Venn diagram is one of the most effective graphic organizers for helping students internalize new information. Gather your class into a large circle and hand out 8½ X 11-inch pieces of construction paper with items to be placed in the Venn diagram. But first, make sure students know what you mean by a Venn diagram. Explain and give examples as needed.

Or—hand out blank pieces of paper and have students write a fact about the topics they have been studying on each piece; collect and shuffle them, and redistribute. Each child receives an item then places it in the correct part of the large Venn diagram outlined on the floor: unique to _____; unique to _____; characteristic of both.

If a student is unsure where a fact should go, offer a lifeline call to a classmate to request some help. After everyone is finished, invite students to step into the diagram and rearrange if one feels an item might be in a better location. This technique shows how individuals think—good information for the teacher—and allows less confident learners a peek into the thought processes of their classmates.

Sometimes classes are just too big or too active for a whole class strategy. Here are two adaptations that might work better for you.

1. Divide the class into small groups. Hand out a stack of index cards and have students write facts or information on each card. Set a minimum number of cards they must complete. Allow one member of each group to gather additional facts from other groups—it's not a competition, but rather an opportunity to think about the information they are studying. You might also seed each group's stack by adding some cards of your own. Then have each group arrange their cards into a Venn diagram. Visit each group and ask students to explain their thinking. When everyone is done, allow students to view the other groups' Venn diagrams. After everyone is seated, ask a few processing questions such as: What similarities did you see among the different diagrams? What differences did you see? or assign a summarizing task such as: Confer with your group and come up with the three most important ideas to remember about this topic.

2. Using a large font, 28 points or larger, make a transparency of the Venn diagram categories: Unique to X, Characteristic to Both, Unique to Y.

   Also in large font on a transparency, list facts about topics being compared and then cut up the items. Place the Venn diagram on an overhead and sprinkle the individual items randomly on top. Invite two students to come to the projector and correctly arrange them in the diagram. Make sure they think out loud and ask for help from the audience.

❑ **Carousel—** This strategy will have students in small groups moving around from place to place while music plays, as in a carousel.

Prepare four or five charts, each with an open-ended review question written at the top. Post them around the room in easily accessible spots. Divide the class into groups of three to five and give each group a different color marker. Rotate groups through all charts. You can track groups by their color. Discuss responses.

• Write chart prompts that suit your purpose for using this strategy. It could be reviewing factual knowledge, preparing students to state and defend an opinion, or having students look for alternative solutions. Write prompts to match your purpose.

- Be prepared to divide the class into groups (e.g. playing cards or color-coded pieces of paper).
- Play music as students rotate to different charts—an easy signal when to move and when to stop.
- Don't leave the students at the charts too long—two or three minutes are enough.
- Keep students active by asking volunteers to read charts at the end of the activity.
- When planning the end of the lesson, think again about your purpose. If reviewing material is the purpose, then just reading the charts and asking for questions might appropriately end the lesson.
- If you want the charts to stimulate a class discussion, have your open-ended questions ready for the discussion after the charts are finished.
- Give students rehearsal time to think about the answers to the open-ended questions. Have them discuss possible responses with a partner.

❑ **ABC charts**— In this strategy you create charts that look like the one below. Each group or set of partners gets a chart with a different set of letters. Go around the class using the alphabet to hear summaries. Making the #3 letter out of sequence helps keep groups attentive because they know they will have to report out again. Here is an example of what this strategy might look like in a social studies class about the geography of Africa.

Arid is a word that describes Africa's desert regions because there is so little water.

Blue Nile is a river in Ethiopia.

Savannas are wide-open spaces with lots of grassland. The Serengeti is a famous savanna.

Congo River is the second longest in Africa.

Dunes are found in the Sahara Desert.

Tanganyika Lake is a big lake.

A digital version of this strategy could be created on a class Wiki, with each chart a separate page of the Wiki. After the pages are shared, students could add information to each other's digital charts.. The originators of each page would be responsible for making sure that the information is accurate. In other words, the students would be creating their own little Wikipedia about African geography. A chart or Wiki page might look like the one below.

Arid is a word that describes Africa's desert regions because there is so little water. The Sahara is the biggest desert in Africa.

Blue Nile is a river in Ethiopia and rises out of Lake Tana.

Savannas are wide-open spaces with lots of grassland. The Serengeti is a famous savanna.

The class then could look online for a school in a country in Africa to contact and ask to verify or add additional information to the Wiki. Perhaps the students from the African school could also add pictures. Together, the two groups of students would be creating a Web resource for other students around the world studying the continent of Africa.

Students can also use images to create their ABC charts. In a math class studying geometry, one might look something like these:

Angles in a polygon must add up to 360°.

Base is the name of the bottom side of a triangle.

Base

Spheres are not polygons.

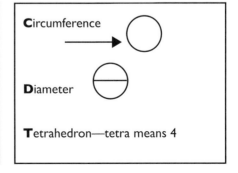

Circumference

Diameter

Tetrahedron—tetra means 4

- Pre-arrange desks in table groups.
- Encourage students to write large enough that the charts are readable from the other end of the classroom. Make a model to share with students.
- Have a way to designate the person from each group who will share (oldest, tallest, longest hair, etc.).

❏ **Tic tac toe**— Divide the class into small groups and give each group nine index cards. On each card they should write a key word or phrase from the unit of study. They then arrange the cards into a tic tac toe arrangement.

Each group writes three sentences: One sentence must include all three words from a horizontal row, one must include all three words from a vertical row, and one must include three words from a diagonal. Groups then pick their best sentences and take turns sharing them.

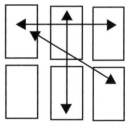

The students hear and talk about the ideas; the teacher can quickly assess what students know and identify any misconceptions that students have (adapted from a Nancy Doda strategy used in a workshop in Boston many years ago).

❏ **Make a choice**— This strategy works well when you want to help students internalize concept such as viscosity or prime and composite numbers. To use this strategy, label sides of the room. For example, when doing viscosity, one side will be high viscosity and the other will be low viscosity. Then give each student a card with an example of the concept on it. The students would decide which would be the correct side of the room for that example and go there (e.g. molasses would go to the high viscosity side).

This should be a non-threatening strategy with students helping each other out—the object is understanding, not catching someone being wrong.

Some concepts for the make a choice strategy are: longitude and latitude; phases of mitosis; metaphors and similes; Union and Confederacy; metamorphic, igneous, and sedimentary rocks; decimals and percents; health facts and myths.

- ❏ **4 corners**— Although Spencer Kagan (*http://kaganonline.com*) created this strategy, it has been been used many times for a variety of purposes. Number the corners of your classroom from 1–4 and give each a different description and a different task. Students choose a corner, go there, and follow instructions such as the following:

  Go to corner #1 if you can clearly explain what a metamorphic rock is.
  Go to corner #2 if you can clearly explain what an igneous rock is.
  Go to corner #3 if you can clearly explain what a sedimentary rock is.
  Go to corner #4 if you can explain all three types of rocks.

  The tasks of corners #1, #2, and #3 are to create a chart that clearly explains the characteristics of each of the types of rocks. The task of corner #4 is to create a graphic organizer that shows the similarities and differences among the different types of rocks. Think about formation, characteristics, appearance, and other factors.

Jill says

This activity gives teachers a quick assessment of who knows what. We can identify any misconceptions and figure out who needs what retaught and who is ready to speed along.

Seven-Day Review Strategies

The following strategies are broader in scope and for use when students have been learning about a topic for a fair amount of time and have much information to process. These strategies require the students to view the information from new perspectives or to apply the ideas in a different context. The seven-day reviews provide opportunities for students to work with concepts in multiple ways, a vital step in mastering new information.

- ❏ **Thumbnail sketches**— I learned about this technique from Martha Rossoll of Topsham and Chebeague Island, Maine. In the art world, students learn to appreciate the details of a painting by isolating and closely studying small sections of the work, often drawing small, detailed pictures of those sections.

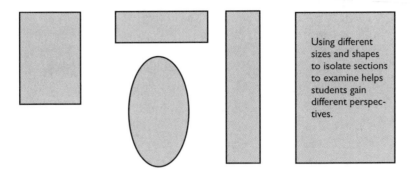

Using different sizes and shapes to isolate sections to examine helps students gain different perspectives.

The same technique can be used with a unit of study or a piece of literature. Students focus on a small section and create a thumbnail sketch that captures the details. These thumbnails can then be used as a framework for a paper, PowerPoint presentation, iMovie, or other multimedia presentation. This technique could be used in these three examples:

- Choose three of the first ten amendments and create a thumbnail sketch for each one chosen that clarifies or illustrates how each amendment protects one of our rights.
- In your group, divide up the steps of mitosis. Each person should create a thumbnail sketch that shows in detail the step he or she has chosen. Assemble your sketches in a mini-portfolio for a presentation.
- Choose a stanza from "Stopping By Woods on a Snowy Evening" and create a series of thumbnail sketches to capture what you visualize when you read your particular stanza.

❏ **Synectics**— Synectics is a strategy designed to make the "unfamiliar" more familiar or understandable by using comparisons. (adapted from Laura Lipton and Bruce Wellman, 2000).

Steps

With students, brainstorm a list of items from their lives—favorite foods, sports, activities, and musical groups. Select one of the items the class brainstormed and prepare a chart that reads _____ (fill in choice) is like _____ because _____

A chemical compound is like chocolate chip cookies because...

Then the class brainstorms all of the similarities of the ones they have identified.

Another version of synectics that students like to do is a visual synectics. Collect 50 + interesting pictures from magazines, postcards, or the Internet. Don't worry about what the subject is; just make sure the pictures are interesting and different from one another. The process is very simple:

- Spread the pictures out and ask a student from each group to choose one that reminds him or her of the topic under study.
- Each student takes a picture back to the small group.
- Student #1 puts his or her picture in the center of the table (all other pictures are face down) and explains its similarities to the topic. A starting sentence might be "This picture reminds me of_____ because . . ."
- Each member of the group then also gets to mention any ways they think the picture is similar to the topic.
- When everyone has spoken about picture #1, each of the other students puts his or her picture in the center, and the process is repeated.

A shorter version may be used when each group chooses one of the individual pictures brought back, and then brainstorms together ways the picture reminds them of the topic under study.

Don't be afraid of synectics because it's different than what you normally do. You will be pleasantly surprised by the creativity and depth of thinking your students demonstrate when using this strategy.

Jill says — Trust the process—it works!

❑ **Blogs**— Blogs, which are Web logs or online journals, are all the rage. You can be set them up for free and monitor them for security and appropriateness. Students respond to your prompts and to each other's responses online. You can use the same requirements you typically use—length, frequency, and others. Posting ideas and responses on the Web allows for a wide exchange of ideas. Blogs also provide an authentic audience that might inspire more thoughtful and accurate responses. Have students find blogs related to topics under study and analyze and research the quality and accuracy of the ideas they find in the blog. Model blogging in class.

❏ **Digital camera**— Many students have digital cameras, so put them to use! A homework assignment might be for students to walk around their homes and find three examples of symmetry; take portrait pictures and write character descriptions based on them; take pictures of an interesting sites and write real-life math problem based on them; or find historical sites in their area that relate to the unit and create photographic essays. All of these assignments ask students to demonstrate their understanding of concepts or processes. Obviously, some students won't have access to digital cameras outside school; so offer alternatives, such as finding images on the Web or in a magazine, or providing cameras and time in school to complete the assignment.

❏ **One-"higher-level thinking" question partner quiz**— Create a question or a problem based on the major concept the class has been studying. Ask students to think about it beyond the literal level. For example: Create a chart that compares one of the reform movements of the mid-1800s (abolition, temperance, women's rights, education) with a contemporary issue (abortion rights, undocumented immigrants, smoking, environment). Think about people involved, tactics, or points of view.

Partners discuss the issues and plan and create a chart to share their ideas with the class. Post the charts. This is a great opportunity to have the class look at all of the responses and discuss why one particular response is strong. Focus on the really strong responses and emphasize exactly what makes them exemplary. This strategy allows students to see exemplars that will help them with future writing assignments. If you have time, allow the partners to revise their charts. This exercise is not done for a grade, yet it provides guidelines for improvement in a low-stakes stress situation while reviewing material. (adapted from Jon Saphier and Mary Ann Haley, 1993)

❏ **Provocative question**— Craft a question that has no "factual" answer. Have students use the facts and ideas they have been studying to develop a position and use evidence to back up their statements.

This strategy can be done orally: *Go to this side of the room if you agree, go to other side if you disagree. Talk with the others on your side of the issue and build your argument to share with the other side.*

This strategy can also be done using chart paper. Divide the class into small groups and have them choose one side of an issue and develop their evidence. Then, students in each group outline their arguments on chart paper, while the class is given an opportunity to respond. This strategy provides a great chance to point out good uses of evidence—students see lots of models before they write independently.

Teach this strategy using a concrete example, such as the one below, with which everyone can relate (TV shows, nursery rhyme conflict, current movie plot conflict).

Evidence for YES	TV shows such as "Survivor" teach valuable life skills	Evidence for NO

Jill says

Groups of students who are not used to sharing ideas are sometimes cautious in their approach to strategies like the ones described in this section. Like anyone approaching something new, they need to develop a comfort level with the new expectations. Be patient and continue to use the strategies, giving students positive feedback as they become more willing to share and work together.

Wrapping it up...

You know that a strategy is worth keeping in your instructional toolbox when it is versatile. You can bring it out in a variety of situations to engage your learners and make them think. The strategies in this chapter work to increase active student participation in a direct teaching situation, and they work equally well when students are involved in an inquiry project, rehearsing for a writing assignment, or completing a reading assignment. Students will internalize new information if they are (1) thinking and talking about it, (2) looking for similarities and differences, (3) summarizing, (4) applying the information in a variety of situations, and (5) reflecting on what they have learned. Sitting through a whole period without movement or interaction is mind deadening. . . . *Ban silent seatwork of more than 15 minutes!*

6...
Reading Is a Social Activity

Interacting with text before, during, and after reading will ensure success.

Students, even good readers, find that strategies they use for narratives do not necessarily work as well with math, science, or digital text. Fortunately we have come to recognize that as students progress through the middle grades they need continuous instruction in reading as print and digital texts become more complex in content and organization. There are excellent books and Web sites that describe what an appropriate middle grades reading program should look like. The strategies in this chapter are for use across curriculum areas, with students interacting with text in two ways— individually and then with other people as the social aspect of reading comes into play.

Interacting with text as an individual reader

❑ **Setting a purpose for reading—** One of the most straightforward ways we can help students become more independent and proficient readers is to set purposes for their reading. Middle grades students struggle with figuring out what is important in a selection. As students read more and more informational text, they find that trying to follow a story line as they do in a novel will not help them figure out what's important in a text organized using cause and effect or problem and solution. By stating a specific purpose and providing graphic organizers or templates that complement text organization, we help students comprehend different types of texts. Here are two examples.

1. Read to find out more about the characteristics of the four types of protista (unicellular organisms) and fill in the graphic organizer with important information on each type..

PROTISTA			
1. protozoans	2. slime molds	3. unicellular algae	4. multicellular algae

Notice how the graphic organizer template becomes a tool students can use to organize new information. Take time to explain to students how their purpose for reading should be connected to their note taking style.

2. Read to find out what problems the pioneers who were traveling on the Oregon Trail experienced and the solutions they used to overcome those problems.

Problem	Solutions
#1 Preserving food	Use dried, salted meat
#2 Broken wheels	Carry tools needed to make repairs en route

This very simple graphic organizer will help students identify which information is critical for their assignment, a skill many students do not yet possess in the middle grades but need to develop.

Setting a purpose for reading and using graphic organizers help students learn to separate in a text what's important and what's not. The goal needs to be that students can independently identify their purpose in reading and what type of graphic organizer will be most appropriate for their task. However, in order to reach that level of independence, most students need to see a lot of teacher and peer modeling of the thinking processes occurring during reading of complex text.

Graphic organizers can be created with the chart function of word processing programs. Students can type information directly into the different blocks or cells and keep the information right on their computers—a boon for students with organizational issues. If a student is using digital text, they can do all of their own work in one place. A modification for some students may be that they simply cut and paste information from digital text to their graphic organizer.

Here's an example of a chart generated by a word processing program:

Type of protista	Protozoan	Slime molds algae	Unicellular algae	Multicellular
Characteristics	*too small to see without microscope *found in water and soil *one cell *herbivores *helps with decomposing	*eat plants that are rotting *used to be called a fungi *range from a few centimeters to 30 square meters		

❏ **Annotate text**— There are a multitude of prompts to use with students when teaching them to annotate. But remember, it's not enough to tell students when they are reading a math problem to underline or annotate the key words in the problem. We need to model the process over and over again and then model it still one more time. We want to invite more and more student participation so that the process eventually becomes automatic.

Jill says

Post-it® notes are great for teaching students how to annotate text. While they can be expensive, sometimes companies have free promotional stickies, or perhaps parents would provide the class with several packages.

Here are three models inviting the students to participate:

- Model #1—*As I read this problem, I'm going to be identify and tell you the key words. Please write them on a Post-it® and stick on the page next to the problem. I will be telling you why I think they are key words.*
- Model #2—*Remember, we're working on identifying the key words in a problem before we start to solve it so that we won't waste time. As I read this problem I see these three words as key words. Why do you think I identified these three words?*
- Model #3—*Let's summarize what makes a word a key word in a math problem.* (Ask for student input and jot it down on the board.) *Okay, using those criteria, I see four key words, and the first one is_____ _____. Who sees a second key word? Why did you choose that word?* Other prompts for annotating might include the following:
- *Use Post-it® notes to keep track of any questions that come to mind as you read, vocabulary that stumps you, connections you make to other topics we've read, or any passages that you find confusing.*
- *At the end of each page, write a one-sentence summary or draw an image that captures the big idea(s) of this portion of the text.*

It is also possible for a teacher to set a specific purpose for students when they are reading digital text. TrackStar (www.4teachers.org) enables a teacher to choose specific Web sites and write an annotation that sets the purpose for reading. TrackStar organizes the selected Web sites, posts them, and sends the creator a URL to give to students. This Web tool is a super resource for differentiation because teachers can post Web sites with different levels of difficulty (lexiles) and assign students to read the one most appropriate. TrackStar also allows you to browse what other teachers have posted or create your own site. The Web site has a number of free tools for both students and teachers to use.

Lisa Hogan of Brunswick, Maine suggests one way to have students annotate digital text is to cut and paste it into a word processing document and have students use text boxes to annotate connections, note questions, or make inferences. Most programs allow text boxes to be filled with a color, so they "pop" in the document. Another way for students to annotate text (thanks to Barbara Greenstone of Brunswick, Maine) is to use *call outs* in the autoshapes part of the draw toolbar in MS Word. An example follows.

> I found Simon Wheeler dozing comfortably by the barroom stove of the old, dilapidated tavern in the ancient mining camp of Angel's, and I noticed that he was fat and bald-headed, and had an expression of winning gentleness and simplicity upon his tranquil countenance. He roused up and gave me good-day. I told him a friend of mine had commissioned me to make some inquiries about a cherished companion of his boyhood named Leonidas W. Smiley—Rev. Leonidas W. Smiley—a young minister of the Gospel, who he had heard was at one time a resident of Angel's Camp. I added that, if Mr. Wheeler could tell me anything about this Rev. Leonidas W. Smiley, I would feel under many obligations to him. —from Mark Twain's *The Celebrated Jumping Frog of Calaveras County*

What's a countenance?

Why did they call the camp Angel's?

When you run short of copies of stories or even novels, or have an inspiration for the next day and need a specific piece of literature, it's sometimes easy and free to download text from the Web. This short story, as well as many other classic stories, are in the public domain and can be downloaded for free. Google *"public domain" + literature* or *"public domain" + speeches*, and you will find a list of sites of downloadable text. Then, check out this site: *http://etc.usf.edu/lit2go/* for free, downloadable MP3 files of children's literature.

Jill says

By insisting that students annotate, we ensure that they are prepared with questions and comments. Whether or not class time should be provided or whether students will do this work at home depends on the specific situation. It won't happen, however, if we don't take the time to model, practice, and coach in class until our students become at ease with the strategy.

❑ **Post fix-up strategies**— This strategy is for an entire team. Teams need to take time to provide explicit instruction on fix-up strategies for students to use when they become confused or lost while reading. Post these strategies, as shown below, in each team room so that students have a resource to check when faced with a problem while reading. Below is a list of strategies from Cris Tovani (2004). Her books provide many ideas for instruction to accompany these strategies. Again, it does no good just to post these strategies— there should be a team plan to model, practice, and coach these strategies.

Fix-Up Strategies

- Try to make a connection between what you're reading and something you already know about from your life or from another book.
- Make a prediction and read to see if it occurs.
- Reread the section.
- Draw a picture that depicts the main idea.
- Retell what you've just read to a partner.
- Identify the text structure—similarities and differences, problem or solution, or cause and effect.
- Trace back to where you got confused and identify what's confusing you: vocabulary, sentence structure, or lack of prior knowledge about something referred to. Try to sort out the problem and ask for help.

(adapted from Tovani, 2004)

Interacting with text and other people

Because most reading problems in the middle grades center on comprehension issues, these active learning strategies can help students understand more fully what they read. Students incorporate such proven strategies as summarizing, non-linguistic representation, and cooperative learning and are provided with opportunities to reflect on and absorb what they have read. We can also use these activities as formative assessments that indicate whether or not students understand the major ideas they have read.

❑ **Fishbowl**— An active way to model, practice, and coach a strategy such as a fix-up strategy is the *fishbowl*. Picture a goldfish bowl with everyone circled around watching the antics of the fish.

- Pick a piece of text that is challenging and easy to divide.
- Divide the class up into groups of three or fours.
- Explain that the class will review what to do when confused by a piece of text.
- Select one of the groups to be the fishbowl and have the rest of the class circle around them.
- Sit with the fishbowl group and explicitly teach them how to use a specific strategy using the first section of the text. Read the text aloud, model your own thinking, and then pull the members of the group into the discussion.
- Stop and process with the entire class. Ask these questions:
  How did we know we were stuck or confused?
  What did you see us do in order to get unstuck?
- Send groups off to repeat the process with section #1 in their own groups. Walk around to coach as necessary.
- Call time and regroup. Ask what the big ideas in section #1 are and put them up on chart paper for further reference.
- Pick a new group with which to process Section #2. Ask for volunteers. *Which group thinks you can model this process with Section #2?*
- Gather everyone around the volunteer group to listen to their process. Ask them to begin ... coach them as necessary ... and process with the entire group asking the question, *How did you know you were stuck? What did you do to get unstuck?*
- Send groups back to work through the rest of the text using the strategies modeled. Walk around to coach as necessary.
- At the end, process with the entire group by placing the big ideas on chart paper and discussing what strategies to use when stuck or confused while reading.

This strategy does take time, but in the end it saves time when students become better independent readers. Caution—one lesson is not enough. If every teacher on the team takes time to do a fishbowl activity with content material, students will receive multiple practices. Imagine how proficient students would become with "fix-up" strategies if both the interdisciplinary teams and the exploratory teams worked together on this endeavor.

❑ **Say something**— This reading strategy takes advantage of the social nature of young adolescents when they work to construct new knowledge from text. Students identify when they are getting lost reading the text chunks and can ask their partner for clarification. Less proficient readers will also hear good readers talk about what they are thinking when they read.

This reading strategy helps you make sense of a piece of text by talking about the ideas as you go along. I will ask you to use these strategies of proficient readers—chunking a text, asking questions, finding connections, summarizing, and making predictions. By working through this strategy you will be prepared for our class or small group discussion.

PARTNERS READING STRATEGY

- Work with your partner.
- Together, chunk up your reading by placing stop signs (Post-it® notes) along the way (unless I have already done this for you).
- Read silently and stop at your stop signs. When you get to each stop sign, talk with your partner about
  —What you think it said.
  —What you think about it.
  —What interests you.
  —What you have questions about.
  —What new thoughts you have.
  —What you might not have understood.
  —How it connects with something else.
- Move on through the reading in this manner until you have finished.
- If you are waiting for others, talk with your partner and decide what three big ideas you think we should discuss as a group or identify questions you want to bring up to the group. If you finish way ahead of everyone else, get some drawing paper and create a visual representation (pictures) of the three important ideas you chose. Summarizing ideas in multiple ways helps us all to think deeply about our reading and increases our learning.

Adapted from www.doe.state.in.us/dps/beginningteachers/supportseminars/english/Say_Something_and_Jig_Saw.pdf

- ❏ **Big idea**— This jigsaw strategy is useful when you just want the students to get the big ideas in a text (adapted from a strategy Nancy Doda uses).
  - Divide text into four sections.
  - Group students in groups of four. Have students in each group number off, 1–4. Student #1 will read Section #1, Student #2 will read Section #2, and so on. This is the home group.
  - Each student is responsible for reading his or her section or paragraph and summarizing the big idea(s) of that section.
  - At this point, you can break the group into expert groups—all the #1s get together and discuss their section, and so on.
  - Home groups reconvene, and each person shares his or her big idea. The whole class hears the big ideas of the entire article.
  - Process the article with the class by asking groups to respond to an open-ended question related to the reading and then have groups share with the entire class.

- ❏ **Collaborative groups**— Begin by selecting a fairly long portion of text that everyone reads individually. Then establish groups to follow these steps:
  - Assign each group a section of the text to summarize on chart paper.
  - Post charts, in order, around the room.
  - Go over the charts together—each group reporting to the class.
  - Provide the groups with an open-ended question to grapple with together. Since they all have read the text, talked about a portion of it, and heard and seen it summarized, they will be prepared for a good discussion.

Jill says

For a change of pace and a tip of the hat to visual learners, have groups come up with graphic summarizers—pictures, symbols, etc. to summarize the big ideas.

❏ **Discussion a là Mr. B's Taxonomy**— This is an Ed Brazee strategy. Prepare a series of questions about an assigned text. Questions 1–5 should be literal comprehension questions; Questions 6–10 should be inferential; and Questions 11–15 should be of a critical, creative thinking nature. After everyone has read the text, divide the class into groups. Each group discusses and answers a question from each of the sets of questions (e.g. 1, 6, and 11) so the group is thinking about the text at three different levels of thinking. Answers go on chart paper or transparencies and are then shared. You can increase accountability by explaining that you expect everyone to be able to explain the answers and will call on students randomly for answers.

❏ **Questions, questions, questions**— The very best questions for taking students deeper into text are their own questions. Divide the class into small groups or partners. Give everyone the reading assignment. If it is printed text, ask them to keep track, either on Post-it® notes or by writing in the margins, of questions that come to mind as they read. If they are reading digital text, have them cut and paste the text into a word processing document. As they read they should type their questions into text boxes. After everyone has finished reading

- Have each group share questions with one another. Using chart paper, record common questions and any others that members want listed on the group chart.
- Share charts; look for similar questions. Note and number them.
- Assign each one of the small groups to answer a common questions and ask them to choose one or two other questions they find interesting.
- Each group then goes back and rereads the text with the intention of responding to the questions.
- Each group shares its responses and should be prepared to point to specific parts of the text where the answer was found, whether it is a literal or an inferential response.

❏ **What should I do?**— This strategy, adapted from a Jeff Wilhelm strategy, explores two different ways to approach a situation or issue and requires that students think deeply about a topic. With literature, you apply the strategy before the students finish the text and know its outcome. When using informational text, use this strategy to summarize, look at alternative outcomes, or review for a test.

- Have students talk with partners or a small group about the pros and cons of taking different actions. The topic might be a dilemma that a famous person or scientist faced. (Don't skip this step!!) (5–7 min.)
    - —*Abe Lincoln:* Fight for Ft. Sumter?
    - —*Robert E. Lee:* Resign his command with US Army?
    - —*Scientist or politician:* Support stem cell research?
    - —*Cell:* Mutate or not?
    - —*Bridge builder:* Suspension bridge vs. arch?
    - —*Juliet:* Continue seeing Romeo?
- Ask for a volunteer to play the role of the character or historical person. His or her job will be to listen to conflicting advice and then make a decision.
- Ask for three or four volunteers to be the "right shoulder advocate"—they are going to try to persuade the character to take a specific action.
- Ask three or four volunteers to be the "left shoulder advocate" —to focus on all of the reasons to take a different action.
- Place advocates on either the right or left side of the character.
- First have a right shoulder advocate give a 30-second pitch for acting in the "right" way.
- Then a "left shoulder advocate" gets to make his or her pitch for 30 seconds.
- Alternate back and forth until all of the advocates have had their 30 seconds.
- Ask the character which side was the most persuasive and why.

Continue reading to find out what the character or person does or what the outcome is. Or, have a discussion focused on if_____ had made a different decision, what might have been the outcomes?

Be sure to emphasize thoughtfulness, accuracy, and evidence as the class debriefs from this activity so that the next time the advocates will be even more persuasive.

To help students feel comfortable with this strategy, do some practice runs with students using situations with which they are familiar.
- Should Jack and the Beanstalk's mom punish him for stealing the golden egg?
- Should Judge Judy send Goldilocks to reform school for breaking and entering?

Don't assume today's young adolescents know old fairy tales —be prepared to retell the story.

Wrapping it up...

Reading in the middle grades is not about word calling or making sure students can identify all of the existing blends and dipthongs. Middle grades reading is about thinking—making connections, predictions, inferences, and synthesizing. Also readers have to practice using different strategies with a variety of texts—print and digital. Our middle grade students need to continue developing these reading skills in each content area in order to master content material. Using active strategies with text helps students develop these sophisticated reading skills through modeling, mentoring, coaching, and clarifying ideas together. ... *Reading is a social activity!*

7...
Rehearse for Success

Rehearsing is a strategy that should be in your tool box. It helps young adolescents overcome "writer's block."

Everyone knows that writing is hard work, and some students need a lot of support when writing. Even when teachers model and provide time to draft, revise, and edit, some students just can't seem to get beyond the blank page. Providing rehearsal time for students before they write allows them to practice using new vocabulary, organize their thoughts, develop their ideas and get beyond "But, I don't want to write today." Here are some strategies.

❑ **Carousel**—Divide the class into groups of three; post chart paper around the room with questions or tasks relevant to the particular piece of writing to be examined.

Write a good open-ing sentence.	What details should be in this piece?	What are the key vocabulary words that need to be in this piece?	Write a good closing sentence.

Have groups rotate through the different charts, offering some ideas that everyone might incorporate into the piece. Take time to reflect on the responses:
- *Did we leave out any details? Important vocabulary?*
- *Which of these suggested opening sentences is most effective? Why?*
- *Which closing sentence would really end the piece well?*

Leave the charts up and help students use them for revision purposes:

- *Go though your paper with a highlighter and make sure you have all of the important vocabulary.*
- *Will any of these details help make your piece stronger?*

As students' confidence grows, the scaffolding, like these charts, can be removed; but it may be a slow process!

Here's a digital version: Set up a Wiki with a different page for each prompt. Group students and have them respond to the prompt on the Wiki during class time. Plug in your LCD projector and review the prompts just like you would the paper charts. The advantage is that your students can access these ideas from home 24/7. You can monitor Wikis by having a notification sent to your e-mail when someone edits a page. It's really pretty easy to add this Web 2.0 tool to your repertoire—your students will help you.

❑ **Walk and talk**— Pair up students, give them a topic to talk about, and have them take a power walk around the building. To keep them honest, build in time for each pair to share the ideas they discussed. Put the ideas on chart paper for reference while writing. Finish the lesson with a quick write where students respond to a prompt based on the walk and talk activity. Quick writes should not be graded; they may morph into a first draft when filed for future use, or become a Ticket Out the Door.

❑ **Chalk talk**— Hang a piece of chart paper or a piece of mural paper on the wall. Identify a topic and invite students to come up by threes and fours and write or draw opinions, ideas, and facts. As more students come up, they can add to the discussion by responding to something already written or by adding something new. Leave the paper up for reference while students are writing. Always take time for students to reflect on what they observe about the ideas on the chart. Some questions you might ask are

- *What do you notice?*
- *What connections can you make between the ideas on the chart and your own experiences?*
- *What are some of the big ideas that emerged?*

❑ **Sound Studio**— See (*http://www.freeverse.com/soundstudio/*), a relatively inexpensive download for Apple computers. Students can record their thoughts, then plug in a set of earphones and play their recordings. As they listen, they can begin to type what they hear. Because their ideas are recorded, they can play them over and over until they are transcribed.

❑ **Inspiration Software**— (*http://www.inspiration.com/*) allows a student to web his or her ideas and convert them to an outline. The outline can be exported to a word processing document and voilà, the student has the framework for the assignment on paper.

Free Web-based brainstorming tools that make webs and other graphic organizers are *http://www.bubbl.us/* and *http://cmap.ihmc.us/download/*

❑ **Music**— Because music is an entry point for some students, have them write song lyrics or a rap incorporating the important information needed for the writing assignment. At this point you need to make a decision—if you just want students to demonstrate that they understand a concept, then you accept the song or rap as the product. If, however, you are also teaching a particular writing genre, then the song or rap will simply be a prewriting strategy. It's important to model for the students how to go from lyrics to a paragraph format. Project the lyrics on a screen and do a Think-aloud about the process you would use to convert lyrics into an essay. In your Think-aloud,
  • Color-code the big ideas and the supporting details that go with each big idea.
  • Identify the order of the ideas and which ones are the most important.
  • Explain how you might use the imagery of song lyrics to help you get a point across to the reader.

❑ **Drawing and cartooning**— Because visual arts are other entry points, suggest students think in images as a prewriting or rehearsal strategy.
  1. Have students fold drawing paper into four or six squares. Students use each square to sketch out a major idea they want to incorporate into their piece. If they chat with someone about the

sketches, they will probably develop more specifics as they talk. Jotting those ideas on the sketch paper will provide a more detailed planning guide. More tactile learners might cut up the paper into the individual squares so they can experiment with order and organization.

2. Comic Life (*http://www.freeverse.com/comiclife/*), another application for the Mac, engages and motivates students' writing as they use digital photos and conversation bubbles.

❑ **5 x 8 index cards**—Some students can't get past the 8½ x 11" blank paper. Help them think in chunks by showing them how to organize their thoughts via 5 x 8 index cards. Card #1 is the introduction that sets the scene; Card #2 explains Point #1 with supporting details (events, people, etc.); Card #3 explains Card #2, and so on. Card #4 should show the most important cause. Be sure to explain why. Card #5 is a conclusion, to restate causes and why #3 was the most important. Make a general statement.

Card #1	Card #3
The American Civil War lasted from 1861 until 1865, but its causes go back to our founding as a nation.	The election of Abraham Lincoln caused the sectional conflict to flare up.

Card #2	Card #4
Sectionalism led to conflict in Congress, among states, and in the courts previous to 1861.	The conflict over slavery dates back to the writing of the U.S. Constitution.

Card #5

The American Civil War only lasted from 1861 to 1865, but its causes and aftermath have stretched across our entire history as a country.

Students outline or jot notes on the actual cards and then use them as they begin writing their first drafts. This strategy may be used with real 5 x 8 index cards or by using text boxes on a computer. Incidentally, emerging research suggests that students who compose on a computer tend to write more.

❑ **Skits**— Divide the class into groups and ask each group to create a skit that incorporates major ideas pertinent to the writing assignment. Be specific in the criteria. Following are several prompts:
- *Your group must show three dangers of early alcohol use.*
- *Your group must demonstrate the transformation of Ebenezer Scrooge.*
- *Your group must demonstrate the characteristics of reflective symmetry.*

❑ **Tinker Toys**— Kinesthetic learners process ideas more easily if they can manipulate objects while they are thinking. Demonstrate building a Tinker Toy construction to help think through the structure of a writing assignments. First model and then coach students through the process. The steps are
- Hold one of the large pieces with multiple holes around the edge.
- Discuss how this piece represents the main idea of your writing. Talk a little bit about the main idea.
- Then, begin to name some major ideas related to your main idea or thesis. As you decide on a major idea, insert one of the sticks in a hole on the main piece and then place a smaller circular piece at the end of the stick. It represents the major Idea #1. Continue to add pieces to represent the major ideas in your writing.
- Next, develop your main ideas with supporting details by grabbing some of the shorter sticks and smallest circular or square pieces. Add them to each major idea piece as you talk about them.

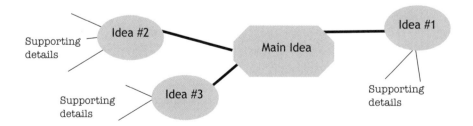

It is easy to identify which ideas need more detail because that part of the structure will be barren. After modeling, have students work together to build a model of their writing piece. They can either record their conversation as they build or one (or a support person) can act as the scribe.

❏ **Card sort**— Have students in small groups, pairs, or individually, brainstorm all the possible ideas for their written piece. Have them lay out the cards in front of them and sort them into categories.

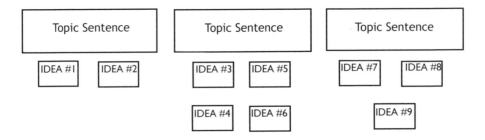

- Next, give students sentence strips on which to write topic sentences. Give out multiple blank strips so students can play around with the sentences until they get ones they like.
- Third step, students organize their groupings in the order that the ideas will appear in the written piece.
- Before students write, have them peer conference on their groupings with the purpose of adding ideas, rearranging details, or deleting unnecessary information.

❏ **Frames**— The teacher provides a physical framework with a structure and prompts for proceeding with the writing (see a sample on p. 79). As students' confidence and skills grow, the teacher withdraws some of the supports from the frame. The goal, naturally, is for students to not need a frame at all.

Frames can be used in any subject. They're a good way to teach the structure of a science lab, an editorial, math journal, a critique of artwork, a reaction to a piece of music, or writing a set of directions. Students working together learn to craft the genre with the use of models, scaffolding, and coaching. Again, the idea is to remove the scaffolding step by step so that students become independent writers. On some state tests, scoring rubrics penalize formulaic writing created by frames, so it is important to help students become independent writers.

Supporting Details	Character Description Frame
Name your character Age_____ Family role_____ Race_____ Character trait #1_____ _____ _____ Give an example of something the character said or did that demonstrates this trait.	One of the most important characters in *Roll of Thunder, Hear My Cry* is _____ _____ _____ One of _____'s most interesting character traits is _____. One way _____demonstrates this trait is when _____ _____ _____ Continue to build the frame until the entire structure is available for the student to use.

❑ **Ranking models**—One strategy to help students develop key writing skills is to have them read and critique multiple models of a specified genre. Here's a strategy that can be used with any genre in any classroom (adapted from a demonstration lesson by Dr. John O'Flahaven, 2002, in Topsham, Maine). This strategy helps students identify the characteristics of a good piece of writing and can be used to create assessment lists with students.

The following steps comprise this procedure:

- Find or write three versions of differing quality of the same assignment, such as a book review, constructed response, lab conclusion, or other.
- Working in small groups, students read the pieces and rank them in order of lowest to highest quality.
- Discuss the rankings with students and come to a class consensus about the ranking.
- Next, ask groups to identify and share the characteristics of the strongest piece. Record their observations on a chart. This chart is the beginning of your assessment list.
- Have students complete a similar piece of writing and self-assess, using the list generated by the class.

- As the class practices this type of writing, students will continue to add to and refine the assessment list.

Following is a model for a social studies open-ended, constructed response question.

DIRECTIONS: Read the following three responses to the following questions and rank them in order based on their quality: 1 = lowest quality, to 3 = highest quality. Be prepared to explain your ranking. These are responses to the following question: Why was trench warfare so hard on the soldiers during WWI? Give at least three specific examples.

A. Trench foot was when soldiers' feet got cold and wet and sometimes they lost them. They got cut off. Also the food wasn't very good. They got shot at a lot too. And gassed. Lots of soldiers died. They did everything in the trenches, ate, slept, fought. Many of the trenches were in France and some soldiers died. The English, German, and French gave the soldiers alcohol. I wouldn't want to be soldier in a trench.

B. Conditions in the trenches were awful for the soldiers during WWI. First the food was unappetizing and as the war went on there was less and less available. By the end of the war the soldiers were living on pea soup with a couple of chunks of horse meat in it. It wasn't enough food to keep them healthy. Secondly, the wet, damp, & unclean conditions led to things like trench foot, body lice and dysentery. Trench foot (foot starts to rot) and dysentery (the runs) could lead to death if not treated. Finally, many soldiers suffered shell shock that caused them to be emotionally upset. Some ended up committing suicide. Life was really tough in the trenches.

C. Life was unbearable in the war. Soldiers had awful food. They had to listen to shells bursting for hours. They got diseases. They only had stuff like canned corned beef and bread to eat. Sometimes they got alcohol. One of the diseases they got was trench foot when they couldn't keep their socks dry, and their feet got wet and infected and sometimes got so bad they had to be cut off. The shells bursting sometimes caused the soldiers to go crazy and do stuff. Their officers thought they were loafing. The bread was made from ground up dried turnips. Lice were another problem, and they caused trench fever. That made them very sick, but didn't kill them. At the end of the war, the soldiers were only getting meat 9 days out of 30. They must have been hungry a lot. It must have been hard to be a soldier in the war.

Students will easily rank example A as the most poorly written with its sentence fragments, choppy sentences, and disorganized presentation. Good conversation will come from identifying the positive attributes of both samples B and C. With subtle questioning from the teacher, students should settle on sample B as the best, even though sample C is longer. Practices like this one allow students to critique and identify writing strategies they can adopt as their own.

Wrapping it up...

Writing itself is hard work. Teaching writing is even more difficult. And it is not, nor should it be, the sole responsibility of the language arts teacher. Each discipline has unique writing requirements, thus students need to practice writing in all of their courses. It's imperative that students be provided the opportunity to practice or rehearse the use of new vocabulary, experiment with strategies for developing an idea in print and digitally, try out different "voices," and test a variety of sentence structures in a quest to be better communicators in the print and digital world. Group work and informal oral presentations are good strategies for incorporating writing rehearsal time into a lesson. .... *Prewriting pays off!*

8...
Master Vocabulary

Word walls are great, but here are strategies to make them fully effective!

"Look up these ten words and write down their definitions."
"Use each word correctly in a sentence."

Please don't ever give those directions again. This type of vocabulary instruction just doesn't help students master new words. However, it is vital that we make vocabulary instruction an integral part of our daily work with students. Vocabulary is key to understanding concepts in the content areas, increasing students' sophistication in reading and writing, and providing them with a spoken vocabulary necessary for personal success in social and work situations (Gregory & Kuzmich, 2005).

Consider that ninth graders from lower socioeconomic situations may enter high school with vocabularies one-quarter the size of many of their classmates! This deficit is a huge disadvantage for students who want to take college prep courses, and we know that in order to have a prosperous life, our current students must have some post-high school education.

Fortunately, recent research studies in word acquisition give us guidelines for making vocabulary instruction effective. Here are several key ideas (Marzano, 2004):

- Students learn new words by internalizing descriptions of the words.
- Students need to demonstrate their understanding of the new word using both graphics and words.
- Students need multiple exposures to a word over time— up to 30 times!
- Teaching students word parts helps them internalize words and their meanings.
- Students need to talk about the words they are learning—use think, pair, shares—and practice using them in different situations.

- Students should play with words in games and puzzles.
- Teachers need to focus on words that will increase students' academic success—words specific to a discipline or words that students won't run across frequently in everyday reading.

Making connections

When teaching vocabulary in the content areas, it is important to emphasize connections of words to major abstract concepts of the discipline. These connections lead to a deeper understanding of the words. Here's an example:

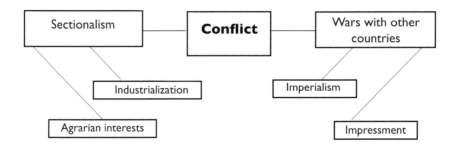

In U.S. History conflict is a major concept. Within conflict there are several major topics and each of those topics has subtopics.

Helping students to understand the relationship between sectionalism, agrarianism, and industrialization and how all three relate to conflict, will assure that they internalize the meanings of these words.

Making connections is one of the ways that we learn, and by making connections among words related to a concept, students build an understanding of the concept beyond a superficial level.

Isabel Beck is a leading expert in vocabulary instruction and its relationship to reading comprehension. According to Beck (2002, 2007), students lacking in vocabulary knowledge will struggle with text because they do not understand the various contexts a word may be used in and are therefore limited in their ability to comprehend text written above a fairly simplistic level. Traditional vocabulary instruction does not help students overcome this deficit and thus students are still unable to comprehend text even though key vocabulary may have been taught before.

Beck divides vocabulary into three tiers:

- Tier 1 contains the most basic words—*table, pet, mother, run*.
- Tier 2 contains "high-frequency words for mature language users" —*crucial, permeate, critical*.
- Tier 3 contains words that are usually found in very specific types of text and rarely in general conversation—*ion, lathe, isthmus*.

Tier 1 probably does not need to be addressed in middle school because students know these words. Tier 3, the content-specific words, must be taught as needed in content areas classes. Tier 2 words, however, need considerable attention because these words appear often in middle and high school texts; not understanding their meaning hampers comprehension of the text and slows down the internalization of new concepts.

Beck suggests the following criteria for determining what words to teach:

- Words not often used in oral language or conversations.
- Words that are sophisticated synonyms for everyday concepts
  — angry = livid or fuming
  — happy = ecstatic or blissful.
- Words that are more apt to be found in writing.

Take a look at these sites with examples of tier 2 words:

- *http://www.uefap.com/vocab/select/awl.htm*
- *http://www.nottingham.ac.uk/%7Ealzsh3/acvocab/awlhighlighter.htm* (will highlight academic words in a selection)
- *http://web.uvic.ca/~gluton/awl/*

The active strategies below reflect that latest research on learning and vocabulary acquisition. They make use of looking for similarities and differences, visual and physical representation, multiple uses, making connections, and play.

❏ **Frayer Model**—This vocabulary strategy can be used in direct teaching, as practice for students individually or with partners. There are four parts to the strategy: definition, characteristics, examples of, and non-examples (Google "Frayer Model" for online sites).

On the following page are two versions of this model:

Model #1   Model #2

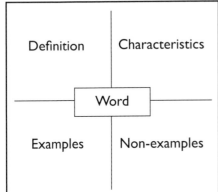
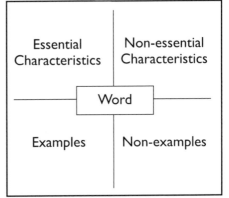

(Hint: When using Model #1, fill in the definition last so that the other three quadrants can be used to help generate the definition. Adding a spot for an illustration also helps students internalize the word.)

The Frayer Model can be used in these ways:

- Preteach new vocabulary in a direct teaching model.
- Review words by having students brainstorm everything they know about the topic and then having partners use these words to fill in the quadrants.
- Use pictures as part of each quadrant.
- Assessment for learning—have individuals fill in a Frayer Model worksheet to check for understanding of a concept. The information received will show whether or not to move on to a new concept or to reteach for more complete understanding.

❏ **Word walls** are popping up all over the country in middle and high schools—they are not just for elementary classrooms any more! A word wall is simply a wall chart of key words in a unit. What is important about word walls is how we use them. Here are some ideas for constructing word walls.

- When possible, have a visual representation of the word next to the written form. Students' retention of a word climbs when linked with a non-linguistic representation.
- Color-code words, because it helps the brain make connections. For example, on a wall chart about photosynthesis and respira-

tion—on a wall chart—color all of the words linked to photosynthesis in one color and the words related to respiration in another color. It will help students retrieve the words later.

- Place words near examples in the classroom. World language teachers often blanket the school with vocabulary words on the real thing. e.g., *le plafond* on the ceiling or *puerta* on the door. A math teacher might have students label all the different types of symmetry within the classroom.

Word walls look good in the classroom; they catch the eye. But they need to be incorporated into the everyday work of the class to be fully effective. Here are some ways to make them more than decorations.

- Use as an end-of-class sponge activity—have students pick a word and give a meaning or use it in a sentence that demonstrates they understand its meaning. This technique can be used as an incentive to go to lunch or to be the first one to get to the bus.

- Begin the class with a review to transition into the work of the day. Ask students to think beyond recall. For example,
  - —*Fred, would you please explain how decimals and fractions are similar.*
  - —*Juanita, which of these words do you think are the most important in our study of changes in our atmosphere and please tell us why.*
  - —*Who can give an example of a TV character who prevaricates as a matter of course?*
  - —*Who can tell me whether a contemporary of George Washington would consider women's suffrage a radical idea?*

- Expand students' vocabulary by posting on a wall a thesaurus of many synonyms, antonyms, Greek and Latin word parts, and word families.
  - —In biology class, there might be a list under the prefix "bio" of all the words the students generated with that prefix.
  - —A language arts teacher might lead the class through a brainstorming activity to generate all the ways to say "said" or "walk" or "pretty or "personality traits." These words are then in plain sight for students to use in their writing. (This idea came from Nancy Rideout, whose Mr. 5 Senses wall display reminded her students to use rich vocabulary in their writing and speaking.)

—A math teacher trying to get across the concept of polygon might combine a word wall list of polygons (and their pictures) with other words that start with poly. Even cooler would be, if the math teacher's teammates posted content words on their word walls that began with the prefix poly and reinforced in multiple contexts the idea of poly meaning many.

- Practice using words correctly while playing with them.
  —*Look at our word wall—I'll give you three minutes to work with a partner to construct a sentence with as many of those words used correctly as possible. Prizes will be given for the most words used and the most complex, grammatically correct sentence.*
  —*In the next few minutes, write a diamante poem, a short rap, or create a picture that demonstrates the meaning of some of our unit vocabulary.*

Jill says

Always try to make these types of activities invitational, by having more than one correct response so that students don't spend time worrying about only one answer you expect.

A word about prizes since I mentioned them above. We all know that students love prizes and that we should use them randomly and not as a bribe for good work. Here's a fun way to award prizes that doesn't cost a cent. It helps if you can be a bit of an actor. When it's time to award a prize, reach down behind your desk and struggle to pull up an imaginary heavy bag. Go through the motions of opening the bag and pulling out possibilities:

Sasha, you have a choice of three fantastic prizes. An all expense-paid trip to Disney World for you and four friends, a $1000 shopping spree in New York City, or a chance to guest star on (fill in a favorite TV show). Which one will you choose?

Believe or not, if done with a sense of fun, the students get into this make-believe world and don't feel cheated by not walking away with a piece of candy or some other little prize. We also learn more about our students by what they choose as a prize. This cool idea was the brainchild of Michael Vasiliauskas, a teacher in Searsport, Maine.

❑ **Action vocabulary**— Divide the class into partners and assign them two or three words they must teach to the class. They may act the words out or use visuals. You can kick this up a notch by not allowing them to use the word and have the class guess it. (Betsy Steen, a former colleague, came up with this strategy.)

❑ **Mix and match**— This strategy works well for reviewing definitions. Create a class set of cards—$1/3$ for vocabulary words, $1/3$ for definitions, and $1/3$ for examples of the words. Color-code them so words are one color, definitions another, and the examples are a third color.

Shuffle the cards and pass them out. Play an energetic tune while the students find their matches. When all are matched, put students in a circle and have the class double check for accuracy.

❑ **Words cards**— Put unit words on index cards and distribute one to each student as they enter the room. If it's at the beginning of the unit, include definitions to help students learn them. If it's at the end of the unit, omit the definitions. Make sure the cards contain both concrete and abstract words.

Here are several great ways to use these cards:
• Students must find a way to work the word into the class discussion in a way that makes sense. Make it a fun contest and keep track of points.
• Use a cloze procedure as a lesson. Put up on the overhead a paragraph with key words left out. As you read the paragraph, pause at each blank and ask who has the correct word to fill in the blank.
• Arrange and rearrange students in small groups and ask them to create a sentence that makes sense using all of the words in their group.
• Have students walk around (play snappy music) and group themselves with other words that go together. Call time and ask each group to share why they grouped together. Play another minute or two of music and have them rearrange in other groups. Call time and ask them to explain this grouping of words.
• Color code the words so that the big idea words (photosynthesis, decimal, coordinate graph, figurative language) are in red and the other words are in blue. Tell the blue words that they must find the red word that they belong to. Call time and have groups freeze and check on each other's physical semantic web.

- Have students create a visual that represents their word. Have them hold up the visual and ask other students to guess what the word is.

❏ **Podcasts**— There are podcasts that focus on vocabulary. Here are two that are amusing and will grab students' attention:
  - *http://www.justvocabulary.libsyn.com* You will receive two words a day as well as hear about idioms and proverbs. The podcasts are archived, allowing students to hear earlier ones. Remember, you don't need an iPod to hear the podcasts, just your computer.
  - *http://learnoutloud.com/Podcast-Directory/Languages/Vocabulary-Building* This site features vocabulary on a variety of podcasts. The *Princeton Review* Minute Vocabulary Podcast is a hilarious demonstration of using words well.

Wrapping it up...

A student's breadth of academic vocabulary is an accurate predictor of that student's future academic success (Marzano, 2004). To ignore vocabulary instruction condemns many students to a frustrating and demoralizing academic career that in turn will lead to diminished economic opportunity. It is educational malpractice when teachers, teams, and schools do not have a stimulating and fun approach to increasing students' vocabulary knowledge! Giving students lots of chances to practice using new words visually, orally, and in writing will help them internalize the many layers of meaning most words possess. ...*Acquiring words is a cool and downright fun thing to do—and it pays off in the future!*

9...
Internalize Concepts

Sounds heavy—and it is, but it is an essential and readily attainable skill.

Concepts can't be internalized by memorizing; they have to be grasped or attained via thinking and refecting. Two useful models for helping students understand concepts are the Concept Attainment Model and the Inductive Thinking Model described in Bruce Joyce and Marsha Weil's classic, *Models of Teaching* (1986). Concept Attainment shows students how to focus on the characteristics of a good example, while Inductive Thinking shows students how to organize bits of information into categories that become big ideas or concepts. Both models give students explicit skills for connecting smaller pieces of information to larger concepts under study.

Concept attainment model

The Concept Attainment Model's purpose is to help students internalize a concept through listing the characteristics that differentiate a good example from a non-example. For instance: What are the distinguishing characteristics of a revolution that make overthrow of the French king a revolution, but not that of another government where coups may happen every six months?

The Frayer Vocabulary Model described in the previous chapter is a good example of an application of concept attainment, but here are ways to introduce the concept attainment model.

- Designate one side of the room the "yes" side and the other "no."
- Explain to the students you are looking for a particular characteristic and that some students have the characteristic and others don't. Their task is to figure out the common characteristics all the "yes" students share.

- In your mind, decide on the characteristic. It must be visible and should go across gender—wearing a watch, wearing something blue, shoes with open toes.
- Point to three or four students and tell them they are a "yes" or a "no." They should move to the designated side of the room.
- Ask the students to try to identify the common characteristic. Don't acknowledge any correct answers at this point. It's all hypothesis.
- Send a few more students to the appropriate side of the room. Ask which hypotheses still hold. Discuss and come to one or two ideas. Ask a student who has it figured out to choose a student to go to the "yeses" or "nos."
- Eventually you must acknowledge which is the right hypothesis.

Take time to link the idea of figuring out what their classmates had in common with identifying the essential characteristics that define a concept and then move into the model using content material.

To begin, here are two ways that involve whole class instruction when you are using this model with content material.

❏ **Defining up front—**
  - Brainstorm characteristics of a particular concept with the class and list them on a chart for future reference. Concept examples are: rational numbers, racism, interdependence, or metamorphosis.
  - Have students individually or in pairs come up with examples to compare to the characteristics or attributes brainstormed.
  - Look at the examples together. Discuss whether the examples are good or not. (This is a time to help students learn how to present evidence to make a case by modeling your thinking in one or two examples.)

❏ **Going in the back door—** This example of a constructive approach helps students understand the different types of literary conflict. The *yes* column reflects examples of character versus oneself conflict, and the *no* column reflects the other types of conflict found in literature.

- Set up two columns on the board—*yes* and *no*.
- The *Yes* column will have all of the items that are examples of the concept and the *No* column has non-examples.
- Start writing examples under the two columns.
- Stop after several and ask students if they can identify the concept you are thinking of.
- Continue to add and discuss examples until you are sure students see the connections between the characteristics and the concept.

Yes	No
Scrooge confronting the three spirits	Cassie & Lillian Jean fighting (*Roll of Thunder, Hear My Cry*)
Pinocchio and his lying	Brian trying to stay alive in *Hatchet*

As students begin to understand the characteristics of the concept you are teaching, ask them to give examples and identify which column they belong in. To end the lesson, have the class generate a list of characteristics of the concept being studied. This list and whatever might be missing will let you know whether or not you need to reteach any aspect of the concept.

This strategy is a great way for students to rehearse what they might write in an open-ended response.

We all need to remember that many concepts seem obvious after teaching them over the years. However, they aren't obvious to students. Take rational numbers—I know, I've studied them—several times. I can't tell you what they are. I wonder: Are they sane? Easy to get along with? Ever become irrational?

Jill says

Don't do a group activity unless you've modeled the thinking.

The concept attainment model can also be adapted for use with small groups. Here are some possibilities.

- Divide the class into partners or small groups.
- Assign groups a different concept from the unit.
- Groups create a short presentation or display where they review the concept for the class, or better yet, present to another class.
- The presentation must include
  - Characteristics of the concept that define it from other ideas.
  - Visual representation of the characteristics.
  - An explanation of how this concept is connected to the unit.
  - Another application of the concept outside the unit being studied.

Inductive thinking model

The Inductive Thinking Model is the other model of teaching described in detail by Joyce and Weil (1986). Inductive thinking takes lots of pieces of information and organizes them into categories from which emerge big ideas. It takes a bit of time but really helps students make connections, draw conclusions, and identify similarities and differences among major units of study within a discipline. Here's a shortened version of the model. Be prepared to spend the class period. Use at the end of a unit to review, prepare for a test, or rehearse for a writing assignment.

- Divide the class up into groups of three or four.
- Give each group a big stack of index cards.
- Provide yourself with masking tape and strips of paper big enough that when you write on them, students will be able to read them from their seats.
- Provide students with an intriguing open-ended question to contemplate as you work through this model. The class will answer the question at the end of the process. For example: *Why were the colonists able to win the revolution against all odds? Knowing what we know about Earth's geological history, what might Earth look like in 10,000 years?*
- Ask the groups to brainstorm everything they can think of related to the unit you've been studying in class (e.g. American Revolution, volcanoes, healthy eating, charts and graphs, *Roll of Thunder, Hear My Cry*, or another topic).
- Ask for students to share what they have written.

- As they share, write each idea on a strip of paper and tape it to the board.
- In small groups, have students copy on their index cards what you are putting on the board—one idea per card.
  At this point you should have a board filled with ideas about the unit. DO NOT organize them as you put them up—that's what the students will be doing. The student groups should each have a stack of index cards with the same ideas listed.
- Explain that you want the students to spread out their index cards and arrange them in groups that naturally go together.
- Model what you mean by arranging a couple of items and explain your thinking. For example, if the topic was the American Revolution, I might group together Ft. Ticonderoga, crossing the Delaware, and Saratoga because these efforts were successful against big odds.
- Give the groups time to organize their cards. The individual index cards help keep the students focused and engaged.
- Walk around and listen; coach when appropriate.
- Ask for suggestions on arranging the ideas on the board. Always ask students to explain their reasoning. This is key because you are trying to develop critical thinking.
- After arranging one group of items, ask if the class agrees that all of these items should be grouped together? Should there be additional items in this group?
- Allow enough time for discussion, but don't drag the process out because you'll start to lose some students' interest. If the discussion is going nowhere, take a vote as to whether a grouping is complete and move on.
- Using the students' ideas, arrange all of the items on the board into groups. Again take time to require students to justify their thinking and to add and subtract items from the groupings.
- Now ask the students to generate labels for each group.

Jill says

It's okay to stop here if you are out of time. The process has helped students make connections and think critically about what they know. The time spent will have helped students internalize the unit information more deeply. If there is time—keep going because the best is yet to come.

- Have students look at the categories with their labels and ask them to process the information with the following questions.
  - What do you notice about the categories?
  - What similarities across the groups do you notice?
  - What differences among the groups do you notice?
  - Any surprises?
  - What things don't you understand? What questions do you have?
  - What additional information might you need in order to answer your questions?
  - What long-range consequences do you see? Any predictions?
  - Then ask the students to go back to the intriguing open-ended question you asked to start the process. Give them time in their small groups to talk about this question.
  - Have the group report its responses to the class.

At this point you will either stop or have students respond individually. In some cases this model is a great way to link different units. For example, if the class studies the ancient civilizations of Egypt, Greece, and Rome, they can look for similarities and differences among the three by comparing charts from their inductive thinking review of each culture. Therefore, it sometimes makes sense to hold on to the charts you make.

This is a complex teaching model, but don't be hesitant to try it. The process engages students and helps them develop a sophisticated thinking process. It will also help them remember information. Now here's a less complicated way to help students solidify their understanding of concepts.

❏ **Matrix**—A matrix is simply a chart for comparing different topics or concepts by identifying specific characteristics of each and which ones they share. Here are two examples.

Matrix Chart #1

Type of rock	Heat involved in formation	Has crystalline layered structure	Changed form
igneous			
sedimentary			
metamorphic			

Matrix Chart #2

Types of volcanoes	Material	Type of eruption	Dangers	Famous example
cinder cone				
shield				
lava domes				
composite				

Certainly, students can partner up to create or fill in a matrix. Discussing which boxes to check helps them clarify their thinking. But we can make it even more active (Rick Wormeli idea) and turn our entire room into a matrix:

- Post the topics or concepts from a unit down one side of the room. Using the previous example, types of rocks would be posted at even intervals down one wall.
- Have students brainstorm the important characteristics that will be used to identify the features of each of the topics. Feel free to fill in any that students omit.
- Post these characteristics at equal intervals across a wall that runs at a right angle to your lists of topics.
- With masking tape, form a matrix grid on the floor.

CHARACTERISTICS

T
O
P
I
C
S

- Ask students to choose a card with a name of a rock on it and then stand in the grid square that identifies both the type of rock and its characteristic.
- Have fun with this strategy and integrate a popular TV game show, such as Deal or No Deal into the process:
  - Allow students a lifeline to ask for help.
  - Have contestants decide whether the students in the matrix are in the correct box—Do they have a deal?
  - Personal best time—how fast can one team get all its players in the correct positions? Change the characteristics and have Team #2 try to beat Team #1's time.

Wrapping it up...

Our students need to develop a mental map of how ideas and concepts are linked in any given unit. They need to see the big picture as well as understand the parts. Daniel Pink, in *A Whole New Mind: Why Right-Brainers Will Rule the Future* (2005), emphasizes this point when he writes about economic success in the 21st century. Jobs that once were thought important and desirable, ones that require only a step-by step process (e.g. legal research, reading x-rays, answering questions about phone service) are being shipped overseas at alarming rates. Economic success for workers in Western countries will rely more on their ability to work across disciplines, to envision the big picture, and to construct a new entity from multiple pieces....*The middle level is the right time to begin developing these more creative, problem-solving capacities.*

10...
Check Progress

Assessing student learning gains—note: I didn't say "testing" or "grading"— must be done often and must focus on the specific skills students are practicing.

Accountability is the big word these days—and as commonly used, it relates to standardized tests. But accountability can enter the picture early as formative assessments are conducted to determine "Are we getting there?" and "What's next?" Dylan Wiliam (2006) uses the term *short cycle* to describe assessments that really make a difference in student achievement. A short cycle assessment is done within and between lessons, day to day, and requires five seconds to two hours.

Wiliam stresses that in order to increase student achievement, we must become adept at using short cycle assessments as part of our instructional practice. He believes this is the most effective type of assessment to improve student learning.

Short cycle assessments

Short cycle assessments tell the teacher whether or not students understand the concepts being taught. Keep these points in mind:

- Teachers need to ask the right questions to get at the deep understanding of a concept, process, or skill.
- The appropriate question requires students to reason out the answer, not just reply with a memorized response.
- It takes time and thought to craft effective questions that can be used across grade level content classes.
- Teachers should collaborate on designing effective questions.

Short cycle assessments also provide teachers with data to make decisions about the next steps in the instructional process. They answer the questions Can I move on? Do I need to regroup and reteach? Do I have to present the information in a totally new way? Here are several examples of short cycle assessing for learning strategies:

❏ **ABCD cards**— Each student has a packet of ABCD cards. The teacher puts a problem or question on the LCD projector or overhead with four possible responses—A, B, C, or D. Students hold up their card(s) to share their responses.

Needless to say, this strategy provides a wonderful opportunity for the teacher to further check for understanding or misconceptions by asking students to explain why they chose particular answers. Wiliam (2006) calls these questions "hinge questions" and gives four criteria for them.
- They focus on important concepts.
- The teacher should plan to use them halfway through the lesson.
- Students should be able to answer them within two minutes.
- Teachers should be able to process the student answers within 30 seconds.

Examples of hinge questions are

Which of these are compound sentences?
  A. The girls were late to physical education class, and they knew they were in trouble because they didn't have a late pass.
  B. Patrick Dempsey grew up in Maine and has become very famous for his role on TV's *Grey's Anatomy.*
  C. The menu in the school's cafeteria has gotten healthier and has been praised in the local newspaper.
  D. The local rock band has won a Battle of the Bands contest; they will now compete in a regional contest in Chicago.

If the students hold up A and D, then you know you can move on. If students hold up other combinations, then you know you must go back and reteach the rules for compound sentences.

Why do we have seasons?
  A. As the earth gets farther from the sun, the seasons change and we have fall and winter.
  B. The tilt of the earth on its axis causes the earth to change its position in relation to the sun.

C. As the earth orbits the sun its tilt on its axis never changes, so sometimes the North Pole is tilting toward the sun and other times it is tilting away from the sun.

D. When either the North or South Pole is tilting toward the sun, the days grow warmer and summer occurs.

If students hold up A, then you know they have not internalized why seasons change. Any other combination also gives you information about the degree of understanding, allowing you to structure the rest of the lesson to ensure student learning.

❏ **Mini-whiteboards**— Each student has a mini-whiteboard to use for a response. Ask a question. Students respond on their whiteboards, and hold up their answers, which can be checked in a visual sweep of the room. Once again, you have information to decide whether or not you need to restructure the next part of the lesson, and your students have reviewed or summarized new learning. If no whiteboards are available, give students a small pad of paper instead.

❏ **One-sentence summaries**— *Everyone grab a marker and write a one sentence summary of what I have explained.* Two minutes later have students hold paper up over their head so everyone can see. It's possible to obtain a quick view of the level of understanding and all students see the main points restated in a variety of ways.

Jill says ● ● ● **Possible idea: Invest in a couple of rolls of cash register tape—you can snip it off easily for students to use for sentences.**

❏ **Webbing**— Webbing, the technique that has become almost standard, not surprisingly can be used in assessment activities.

- At the beginning of a unit or reading assignment, have each student web what he or she already knows about the topic. Make sure students use just one color of marker. Collect and keep safe for future use.

- To check understanding as the unit progresses, pass out the webs, and have students add new knowledge and revise any misconceptions they can identify. This time the students should use a second color marker. Collect and review the webs for a quick check of student understanding. Make revisions to your instructional plan to meet students' needs.
- At the end of the unit, pass out the webs once again. Have students use a third color to add new knowledge about the topic. Have students reflect on what they have learned. This strategy is a great visual representation for students of all they have accomplished. Collect and make a final review to see if there is anything you need to reteach before the final assessment.

Providing feedback

Another aspect of formative assessment that Wiliam emphasizes is that feedback must be given to the learner and that it needs to provide guidance as to what next steps the learner should take to continue to improve. Most strategies for feedback include conferencing with peers and the teacher. Below are two such strategies to use with partners.

❏ **Assessment list with next steps**— Students pair up to look at each other's work using an assessment list developed as a class. As they check off the criteria that have been met, they also annotate where in the text the author has met the criteria.

It might be done with Post-it® notes, a specific highlighter, or just notes in the margin (adapted from Anne Davies).

Criteria	Where Met	Next Steps
Xxxxxx	_____	_____
Xxxxxx	_____	_____
Xxxxxx	_____	_____
Xxxxxx	_____	_____

Then together the partners discuss what the next steps are for the author to meet all of the criteria, and those notes are jotted down in the column labeled Next Steps. Then the partners repeat the process for the other partner's piece. Using feedback, students improve the quality of their work before a final assessment. This same process could be used for a science lab or open-ended math problem requiring a constructed response.

❑ **Stoplight**— Students receive red, yellow, and green dots. When they peer edit or assess, they use the green dots to indicate which parts of the piece are meeting the standards described in a rubric, yellow dots to show which parts are close but still need some work, and red ones to mark those sections that do not meet standards. Students also jot down or share aloud suggestions for improvement. The color-coding gives the student immediate feedback on where to focus their attention (Dylan Wyliam strategy).

Wrapping it up...

Assessing for learning is a powerful instructional practice that impacts student learning. Research suggests that assessing for learning is one of the most powerful tools teachers have for increasing student achievement (Wiliam, 2006). We do not need to rely on the big publishing companies to define and distribute our formative assessments. There are active learning strategies that work really well as formative assessments to provide instantaneous and accurate feedback on the depth of the students' understanding of our lessons. However, these tools will only be effective if we make intentional adjustments to our instructional plans based on the data. Students must also receive this feedback accompanied by specific next steps they need to take to improve their work before the final assessment. . . . *Let's take the guesswork out of learning!*

11...
Create Connections

Help students connect the dots so they can see the big picture.

Students need to make connections among the various units they study so they see that events, trends, and actions do not occur in isolation, but are interconnected. They need to develop their abilities to discern causal relationships, identify similarities and differences, make predictions based on evidence, and thus become systems thinkers ready to meet the challenges ahead. The strategies described below work well in helping students connect ideas, themes, and concepts across units.

Overarching questions or conceptual frameworks

Providing specific links among units that relates lessons learned in a previous unit to a current unit or one to come this quarter or semester helps students make connections, predictions, and inferences. Using an organizing structure like a broad question or generalization or concept is a good way to get students to practice these types of thinking.

❏ **Overarching questions—** Google "essential questions" or "overarching questions," and excellent sites pop up with guidance for crafting these open-ended questions, which require critical thinking to answer. Usually these sites focus on questions for a unit. However with a little bit of thought, it is possible to develop questions that stretch across a quarter or a semester. Here are several examples of overarching questions:
- How has technology impacted cultures?
- How are math concepts applied in everyday life?
- How do cyclical patterns shape our earth?

Generalization as a conceptual framework

In *Concept-Based Curriculum and Instruction: Teaching Beyond Facts,* Lynn Erickson (2002) lists four characteristics of generalizations:

- Broad and abstract
- Timeless—applicable in the past, present, and future
- Universal—apply to different cultures and time periods
- Examples vary but always hold up under scrutiny in supporting the generalization.

Generalizations are easy to find in any subject, theme, or unit. Here are three examples:

- The similarities and difference among immigrants to the U.S. have led to both conflict and collaboration.
- Mood can be created with words, music, and images.
- The loss of biological diversity will affect the economics, health, and sustainability of the global community.

Concepts are also abstract, universal, and timeless. They, however, can be stated in one or two words and share common characteristics. Examples of concepts include patterns, systems, structures, and conflict.

Post the question, generalization, or concept in a highly visible location in the classroom. Refer to it often and work it into lessons occasionally.

Questions, generalizations, and concepts each allow the class to connect the dots across units and ask penetrating questions which compare, contrast, evaluate, synthesize, and produce new thinking. However, these linkages and thinking processes should not be delivered in lecture format. Have students work hard to do the thinking, with coaching and necessary course corrections provided as needed. Here are several ways to engage students in collaborative activities that help them make connections across units.

❏ **SEEing the connections**— Create a graphic organizer that lists the units of the semester. After each unit, ask pairs or small groups to students to fill in the appropriate column with words and images that capture the big ideas that relate to the question, generalization, or concept. Assign each group a wanderer whose job it is to visit other groups and chat with them about their ideas. Wanderers bring back to the groups the ideas heard around the room. With the input on all the other groups' ideas, everyone is making connections to the unit. This strategy is about collaboration rather than competition; the idea is to reinforce new learning. As the semester moves on and units are added, students acquire a new graphic organizer.

- After each unit have small groups look at all of the graphic organizers generated by the small groups. Direct the students to look for patterns.
- An organizing question for the work might be, "What patterns do you see across the three units? How many similarities can you find?
- Hold the groups accountable by having them report to the entire class.
- Help individual students reflect on what they find through journal entries, quick writes, or quick draws.

Here's an example of what a group might report after looking at their graphic organizers.

How Has Technology Impacted Cultures?

Europeans in the Age of Exploration	Indigenous peoples of North and South America had no defense against European guns—defeated	U. S. in Industrial Age
Compass rose		Steamboat expands transportation
Astrolabes		Farmers can sell crops to more people
Improve navigation		

- ❑ **Database**—Teach students how to set up fields in a database and record pertinent information. As students add to the database during each unit, they can sort and organize the information in the database and look for patterns. Images as well as text can be used in databases.

How Has Technology Impacted Cultures?

Invention	steam engine
Culture	England/Europe
Impact #1	factories could make more goods
Impact #2	more people moved from farms to city

❑ **Identify similarities and differences among units studied**— Marzano, Pickering, and Pollock (2001) list identifying similarities and differences as one of the nine instructional strategies that research has shown to be effective in increasing achievement. A double-bubble graphic organizer is similar to a Venn diagram. It identifies those characteristics in units that are common among topics and those unique to each. The illustration below compares and contrasts the colonization of North America with the colonization of Africa. The visual representation allows students to quickly see what was similar and what was different in the two events.

Sometimes bigger is better, simply because it is easier to see. Think about using sidewalk chalk and going outside to the parking lot to make your double bubbles. The students could plan their giant-sized graphic organizer inside and then go outside to execute it.

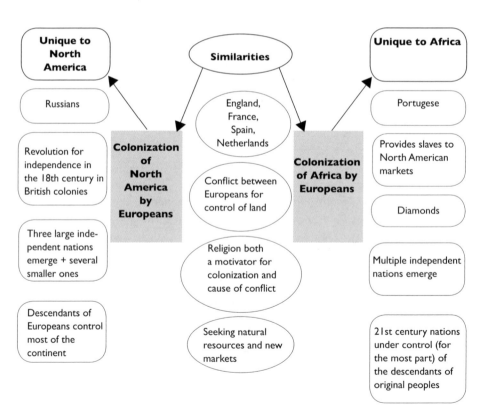

❏ **Museum gallery**—This strategy is a visual review of the major events or concepts that stretch across units. Small groups or partners will create a museum exhibit around a theme following this process.

- Gather many different art supplies for students to use.
- Think about the units that have been studied and brainstorm the different combinations of possible exhibits. For example, if there have been three units called A, B, C then some possibilities include:
  – Information unique to A
  – Information unique to B
  – Information unique to C
  – Information common to A & B
  – Information common to A & C
  – And so on
- Some of the combinations need to be repeated because there should be as many as the number of groups in the class.
- Write the combinations on slips of paper and put them in a box.
- Each group draws a slip from the box. Group members must create an exhibit using the art supplies that fit the description on the slip they drew.
- Each group goes through a thought process that identifies both the critical information it must include and the information that must be eliminated because it doesn't fit the criteria for the exhibit.
- When the exhibits are finished, each group chooses a docent, a person who leads tours through a museum, who will stay at the exhibit to explain and answer questions.
- Other group members tour the other exhibits.
- At the end, a time of reflection occurs as the class reconvenes to consider some guiding questions that will help them synthesize what they saw and heard.
  – What are three big themes we saw that occurred in each unit?
  – Which unit seems to be the most unique? Why?
  – What are the biggest differences you saw?
  – Are there any cause and effect relationships among the ideas in the units?
  – What might you predict about our next unit on_____?

Wrapping it up...

Life is not arranged in unique, little blocks; it doesn't follow an outline like a class unit. Even disciplines are no longer categorized by simple labels. Biology is now biochemistry, biophysics, and biometrics. Creative and critical thinkers have to be able to look beyond their own field for inspiration and problem-solving strategies. This ability to think divergently as well as convergently does not occur magically when an advanced degree is achieved. We must have our students looking for connections and themes early on so that they can train their minds to be receptive to innovative solutions to the challenges they will face. Middle level advocates have been pushing for challenging and integrated curriculum since the beginning of the middle grades movement; perhaps it's time to really listen to them. Even if we can only orchestrate this type of approach within the four walls of our classrooms, thinking and working across units and disciplines need to be critical attributes of our lessons. Fortunately, the resources of the Internet make it easier to achieve this goal. Read Brenda Dyck's (2004) *The Rebooting of a Teacher's Mind* for inspiration on incorporating the possibilities provided by the Web as a way to integrate lessons. . . . *Schooling shouldn't be done solely by subjects, because life certainly isn't!*

Before You Leave...

You accepted the invitation this book offered to learn more about engaging instructional strategies. You were introduced to examples, strategies, and activities. Now, before you put this resource temporarily aside, take a few minutes to put it all in perspective. Visualize the classroom scene described just below, reflect on what is happening, identify the key characteristics, and perhaps then find a metaphor that captures the essence of what goes on in your little corner of the universe where young adolescents learn and grow.

Small groups of students bend over a picture while others gather around a computer screen, talking surprisingly softly as they try to answer questions they generated while previewing materials for the new unit. Elsewhere in the room, students are reading while others are hard at work creating an iMovie they will use to demonstrate they understand a concept under study. It's hard to immediately find the teacher until he asks everyone to focus on him so they can take a few minutes to review what they have learned during the first part of the class.

Asking each group to fold a piece of chart paper in thirds, he then asks the class to list or draw a representation of three important pieces of information they have been studying in the top third of the chart, write any questions they have in the mid portion of the chart, and to list their next steps in their project on the bottom third of the paper. After a few minutes, he has the groups hold up their charts and share. Several things became apparent during this sharing: (1) the teacher quickly checked on each group's progress; (2) all students heard multiple summaries of the information under study, and the teacher identified any misconceptions that need to be corrected; (3) the teacher noted the students' questions in order to plan upcoming direct instruction; and (4) students planned and managed their own time by identifying their next steps, thus continuing to internalize a process for self-directed learning.

Glancing around the room, it is obvious that each student knows what to do and feels comfortable sharing ideas as well as asking questions about content and processes. The classroom is one where everyone feels invited to participate and learn in his/her own way.

Such a classroom is not simply the result of linking together several activities where students hop up and down and cross the room to chat with one another about the day's topic. It is instead a dynamic mix of carefully crafted learning experiences that rest on a foundation of respectful and caring relationships between students and their teacher. Secondly, the curriculum or the material to be studied must be relevant to the students' lives as well as challenging and engaging. Taking time to forge the links between the interests of the students and the requirements of the curriculum pays off for those students who have been reluctant to invest their energy in studying information and ideas that appear irrelevant to their lives. Relevance is a form of invitation.

Finally, a well-crafted learning experience is a result of a teacher's thoughtful choice of instructional strategies designed to help students discover relationships among ideas and practice skills they will apply in other situations. Because the strategies require creative thinking and active participation, students cannot glide through class by regurgitating memorized facts or hiding under their hoodies in the back of the room. These strategies also allow the teacher to continually monitor student understanding, thus assessment for learning is skillfully woven into the process.

Do you remember the Hans Christian Andersen fairy tale about the Little Match Girl? The childhood image I have from this sad tale is of a little girl imagining happy scenes that she will never experience. No classroom should ever have "Little Match Girl" students who feel they are left out of the learning, always looking in at others who seem to "get it" and are thereby successful while they sit wondering what's wrong with them.

As teachers we have tremendous power to influence our students' sense of self in terms of their confidence and competence, key factors in ensuring that each student feels invited into the learning process. Our words, expressions, and lesson delivery all have an impact. Words that always point out the deficits instead of building on strengths, looks that express disappointment instead of encouragement, lessons that continually ignore learning needs send powerful messages to students that they aren't good enough, don't deserve to be inside. Students on the outside looking in rarely learn.

An awesome responsibility goes hand and hand with this power. A responsibility to be thoughtful and creative in our planning if we are to ensure that there are no Little Match Girls or Boys in our classes. I would never suggest that merely stringing together a series of active learning strategies described in this book would increase learning. Rather, my hope is that this book will be a resource for planning and will help many teachers find ways to

- Connect students with the curriculum by accessing or developing prior knowledge that entices the students to want to know more.
- Use instructional strategies that take advantage of learning strengths.
- Allow students to explore ideas about the world.
- Create non-threatening situations where students can rehearse new ideas and practice skills without fear of a low grade.
- See 21st century technology as an integral component on the learning process and not just a novelty.
- Ensure students are doing the thinking and generating the questions that keep units intellectually stimulating.
- Use formative assessments to identify when things aren't going well for the students and to alter the instructional plan in order to address these needs before the final assessment.
- Create a classroom where everyone is working hard while enjoying themselves and where no one feels left out.

Metaphors are effective learning devices because they create powerful imagery to denote an idea or concept. I invite each of you to create a positive metaphor that captures the essence of the classroom you want to create, a place where each student feels invited to participate, has confidence to share and ask questions, and collaborates with classmates. Some may see a marching band where multiple musicians make stirring music together, others may envision the classroom in terms of an intricate quilt of many different pieces of fabric pieced together, or still others might see a chef concocting a delicious dish out of seemingly unrelated foods. All of these metaphors suggest that the whole is greater than the sum of the individual components. The classroom where everyone is invited is artfully designed.

I will end with *my* favorite metaphor, a piece of Maine middle level lore. Sandy Caldwell was principal of the Middle School of the Kennebunks and a middle level pioneer in Maine. Her words spoken then still resonate today. "In our school everyone has a first class ticket. No one rides coach." *... Let's find a way to eliminate second-class learning for each of our young adolescents and ensure that every student is invited to ride first class through the middle grades.*

Fantastic Resources for Putting Zip Into Your Lesson Plans...

Sites about active learning
- **http://www.portaportal.com** (guest name: Spencer)
- **http://www.teachtech.ilstu.edu/additional/active.php** Center for Teaching, Learning, and Technology
- **http://www1.umn.edu/ohr/teachlearn/tutorials/active/index.html** Center for Teaching and Learning, University of Minnesota

Books with activating and summarizing activities
- **http://www.rbteach.com/rbteach/pubs.asp** Jon Saphier and Mary Ann Haley *Activators* (Research for Better Teaching) *Summarizers* (Research for Better Teaching)
- **http:www.ascd.org** Rick Wormeli, *Summarization in Any Subject* (click online bookstore)

Other Books by Rick Wormeli
http://www.stenhouse.com/html/titlesbyauthor. htm#W

- *Meet Me In The Middle: Becoming an Accomplished Middle-Level Teacher*
- *Day One and Beyond: Practical Matters for New Middle-Level Teachers*
- *Fair Isn't Always Equal: Assessing and Grading in the Differentiated Classroom*

Books by Jeff Wilhelm
http://www2.scholastic.com/browse/
(search for Jeff Wilhelm)

- *Action Strategies for Deepening Comprehension*
- *Engaging Readers and Writers with Inquiry*
- *Improving Comprehension with Think-Aloud Strategies*

Blogs

- **http://www.learningcircuits.org/2002/apr2002/ttools.htm**
  An overview of blogging.
- **http://www.blogger.com/** A site for setting up a blog.
- **http://www.middleweb.com/mw/aaDiaries.html**
  Middle School blogs.
- **http://www.glencoe.com/sec/teachingtoday/weeklytips.
  phtml/** Teaching Tips from Glencoe/McGraw-Hill publishers.

Software

- **http://www.freeverse.com/apps/app/?id=5011** Comic Life
  (create comic strips, graphic novels, projects that demonstrate
  learning).
- **http://www.inspiration.com/** Inspiration software (create webs
  with both words and images; easily converts to an outline and then
  can be exported to a word processing document).
- **http://www.aquaminds.com/** NoteTaker (NoteShare) (digital
  spiral notebooks that can be shared via a server; text, video, images,
  sound files can be added.
- **http://www.earth.google.com/** Free download of maps and
  satellite images for complex or pinpointed regional searches.

Foldables

- **http://www.dinah.com** Folding paper to make graphic organizers.

Online graphic organizers

- **http://www.eduplace.com/graphicorganizer/**
- **http://www.graphic.org/**
- **http://www.teach-nology.com/web_tools/graphic_org/**
- **http://www.sdcoe.k12.ca.us/score/actbank/torganiz.htm**
- **http://www.teachervision.fen.com/page/6293.html**
- **http://www.longwood.edu/staff/jonescd/projects/
  educ530/aboxley/graphicorg/fraym.htm** (Frayer Model)

Podcasts

- **http://www.apple.com/itunes/store/** Podcasts on all sorts of
  topics.
- **http://www.NPR.org** National Public Radio podcasts.
- **http://www.podcast.com./** Alphabetical listing of podcasts.

- **http://www.mabryonline.org/podcasts/** Podcasts from Mabry Middle School in Georgia.
- **http://www.epnweb.org/** Education Podcast Network
- **http://www.apple.com/quicktime/tutorials/videopodcasts. html** Tutorial for making a podcast on a Macintosh computer.

Portaportal sites

http://www. portaportal.com is an easy way for teachers to post sites for their students. Below is a list of guest names that open portals—explore!

- greenstone (an eclectic mix of sites)
- spencer (lists a variety of middle level curriculum and instruction sites)
- christoy (another eclectic middle level site)
- maineliteracy (literacy issues)
- universalelements (literacy sites)
- camdenhills (middle level topics)

Videos

- **http://www.Youtube.com/** People post all manner of videos to this site. You can search by topic, and often you will find something that helps students understand a skill or concept.
- **http://www.teachertube.com/** TeacherTube is similar to You-Tube in that teachers post videos from their classrooms: demonstrations, student work, discussions, and other resources.
- **http://www.Video.AOL.com** Funny videos that might help you make a point in class.
- **http://www.zamzar.com/** This site allows you to convert an online video from YouTube or other site to a format that you can save to your desktop. This service is extremely useful to teachers because schools often block access to YouTube and other video resources. Access and convert the video at home and use in your classroom without having to go back out online.

Wikis

Two free Wiki sites where you can create a class Wiki to post assignments or facilitate online discussions.

- **http://www.wikispaces.com/**
- **http://pbwiki.com/**

References...

Atkinson, C. (2005). *Beyond bullet points: Using Microsoft Powerpoint to create presentations that inform, motivate, and inspire.* Seattle: Microsoft.

Beane, J. (1993). *A middle school curriculum: From rhetoric to reality.* Columbus, OH: National Middle School Association.

Beck, I. (2007, November). *Rev up Instruction in the middle grades.* Presentation at the annual conference of National Middle School Association.

Beck, I., McKeown, M., & Kucan, L. (2002). *Bringing words to life: Robust vocabulary instruction.* New York: Guilford Press.

Brain Connection (n.d.) Retrieved July 22, 2008, from http://www.brainconnection.com/

Christen, W., and Murphy, T. (1991). Increasing comprehension by activating prior knowledge. ERIC Clearinghouse on Reading and Communication Skills. Retrieved February 21, 2007, from http://www.ericdigests.org/pre-9219/prior.htm (ERIC Identifier: ED328885)

Daniels, H., and Bizar, M. (2005), *Teaching the best practice way: Methods that matter, K-12.* Portland, ME: Stenhouse.

Gregory, K., Cameron, C., & Davies. A. (2001). *Conferencing and reporting.* Merville, BC: Connections Publishing.

Erickson, L (2002). *Concept-based curriculum and instruction: Teaching beyond facts.* Thousand Oaks, CA: Sage.

Gregory. G., & Kuzmich, L. (2005). *Differentiated literacy strategies for student growth and achievement.* Thousands Oaks, CA: Corwin Press.

Jensen, E. (1995). *Brain-based learning.* San Diego, CA: The Brain Store.

Kagan, S. (1992). *Cooperative learning.* San Juan Capistrano, CA: Kagan Cooperative Learning.

Kuzmich, L. (2007, July). *Level II literacy training: Increasing student success.* PowerPoint Presentation, Colby College, Waterville, ME.

Leahy, S., Lyon, C., Thompson, M., & Wiliams, D. (2005). Classroom assessment: Minute by minute, day by day. Retrieved June 26, 2008, from www.state.nj.us/njded/nj-pep/classroom/arts_assessment/worddocs/ClassroomAssessment.pdf

Lipton, L., & Wellman, B. (2000). *Pathways to understanding: Patterns and practices in the learning-focused classroom.* Sherman, CT: MiraVia.

Joyce, B., & Weil, M. (1986). *Models of teaching* (3rd ed.). Englewood Cliffs, NJ: Prentice-Hall.

Marzano, R. (2004). *Building background knowledge for academic achievement: Research on what works in schools.* Alexandria, VA: Association for Supervision and Curriculum Development.

Marzano, R., Norford, J., Paynter, D., Pickering, D., & Gaddy, B. (2001). *A handbook for classroom instruction that works.* Alexandria, VA: Association for Supervision and Curriculum Development.

Marzano, R., Pickering, D., & Pollock, J. (2001). *Classroom instruction that works: Research-based strategies for increasing student achievement.* Alexandria, VA: Association for Supervision and Curriculum Development.

National Middle School Association. (2003). *This we believe: Successful schools for young adolescents.* Westerville, OH: Author.

National Middle School Association. (nd). Fundamentals of student success. Retrieved June 26, 2008, from http://www.nmsa.org

Pink, D. (2005) *A whole new mind: Why right-brainers will rule the future.* NY: Penguin Group.

Roschelle, J. (1995). *Learning in interactive environments: Prior knowledge and new experience.* Retrieved February 22, 2007, from http://www.exploratorium.edu/IFI/resources/museumeducation/priorknowledge.html

Saphier, J., & Haley. M. (1993). *Summarizers.* Carlisle, MA: Research for Better Teaching.

Scieszka, J. (1989). *The true story of the three little pigs.* New York: Viking.

Sprenger. M. (2005). *How to teach students to remember.* Alexandria, VA: Association for Supervision and Curriculum Development.

Tovani, C. (2004). *Do I really have to teach reading? Content comprehension, Grades 6–12.* Portland, ME: Stenhouse.

Wilhem, J. (2002). *Action strategies for deepening comprehension.* New York: Scholastic.

Wiliam, D. (2006). *Using assessment to support learning: Why, what and how?* -PowerPoint Presentation retrieved June 26, 2008, from http://216.239.51.104/search?q=cache:zpcvxS7nMTEJ:www.maine.gov/education/presentations/dylanwiliam122006.ppt+%22dylan+Wiliam%22+%2B+stop+light&hl=en&ct=clnk&cd=3&gl=us&client=firefox-a